ACTIVATING
the
Gifts
of the
HOLY
SPIRIT

ACTIVATING the *Gifts* of the HOLY SPIRIT

DAVID IRELAND

Whitaker House

ACTIVATING THE GIFTS OF THE HOLY SPIRIT

David Ireland
Impact Ministries International
68 Church Street
Montclair, NJ 07042
(973) 783-1010

ISBN: 0-88368-484-5
Printed in the United States of America
Copyright © 1997 by Whitaker House

Whitaker House
30 Hunt Valley Circle
New Kensington, PA 15068

Library of Congress Cataloging-in-Publication Data

Ireland, David, 1961–
    Activating the gifts of the Holy Spirit / by David Ireland.
        p.   cm.
    Includes bibliographical references.
    ISBN 0-88368-484-5 (trade paper)
    1. Gifts, Spiritual.   I. Title.
    BT767.3.I74   1997
    234'.13—dc21   97–40024

1 2 3 4 5 6 7 8 9 10 11 12 / 07 06 05 04 03 02 01 00 99 98 97

Contents

Introduction

I can't remember a time when I didn't have my heart and mind set on becoming a mechanical engineer. The three boys in our family devoured every copy of *Popular Mechanics* that my dad brought home for us. We were continually taking apart everything we could put a screwdriver to and then trying to put all the parts back together again.

I began college as a sixteen-year-old with the goal of having my Ph.D. by age twenty-five. Before we knew it, my younger brother and I were indeed graduates and practicing engineers. I, David Ireland, however, the radically left-brained cynic, wound up about as far off course from his original intention as anyone could have ever imagined. I found myself being enlisted by the Lord for a spiritual journey that took a hard turn away from where all my natural and intellectual inclinations had been taking me all my life.

For a couple of years when we were growing up, once a week we all got dressed up and went to a liberal church not far from our house. A few hymns, a twenty-minute sermon on some moral topic, and we were out the door to do whatever we wanted. If I ever heard a salvation message, I don't remember it. Then again, I wasn't paying much attention. We stopped going when I turned twelve, and from that point onward I had no biblical or Christian influence in my life. Soon I stopped believing there was a God and became a teenage atheist. "Show me God in a test tube, and I'll believe," was my motto.

At Fairleigh Dickinson University in Teaneck, New Jersey, where I did my undergraduate work, I came to be known as the guy who gave Christians a hard time. People didn't have to find me to share their faith; I'd go find them. Eventually, Christians would see me coming and walk the other way. In many ways I was like the apostle Paul, who was so anti-Christian that he did everything he could to persecute believers.

I didn't go out of my way to specifically study anti-Christian literature. I had developed arguments on my own because, in truth, I was really searching for God. But I didn't know that at the time and surely would not have told anyone if I did. You see, I looked down on Christians with prideful contempt because I did not consider them my intellectual peers. It was my opinion that most of the Christians I had met had simply made emotional decisions to convert.

All this time there was a growing void in my life. I kept asking myself, "What do I do after I get all the education I can get? What do I do when I get all the money I want? Where does life take me then?"

I think people who argue the most are often the ones who are really searching. That's why they have such a strong conviction about their positions. I was arguing, hoping to find some answers. My arguing lasted for approximately two years, and I became really frustrated with life. I was now ready to listen to and entertain the idea of the existence of a God who loved me.

At 10:00 P.M. on July 6, 1982, at the age of twenty, I wholeheartedly accepted Jesus Christ. The next day I started sharing my faith and, shortly thereafter, I led a number of my fellow students to the Lord. To say the least, old friends were very surprised. Some of the non-Christian ones began calling me "Reverend" in a joking way. When I first went to church, a number of students from the campus in the congregation seemed quite nervous. They thought I had followed them to the worship service to publicly antagonize them. They could scarcely believe that I had given my life to Jesus.

I had never met anyone who talked about or demonstrated the power of the Holy Spirit. I didn't even know it was an issue. I was one who had *"not even heard that there is a Holy Spirit"* (Acts 19:2). I soon started attending a full gospel church that taught about the gifts of the Holy Spirit and the power of God. As I read the Bible and saw the power of the early church, I longed to experience those same things. I started praying and fasting for God to do that in my life, too.

Again, I had a lot of questions. How could I speak in an unknown tongue, having never studied languages? But by then I had quit fighting. I read the Bible and accepted it in its entirety. About a month after salvation, I received the baptism of the Holy Spirit. Now the same Christians who were afraid of me because I argued with them, were now afraid of me because I began moving in the gifts of the Spirit.

My spiritual journey had brought me from being a skeptical, analytical atheist to being a born-again, Bible-believing Christian. One might have guessed that I would have become a Christian apologist. I do indeed love apologetics. We should have reasonable ways to defend the authority and authenticity of the Scriptures. But I had become a Christian, not because I finally met someone who could answer all my questions, but because my heart was open and hungry for God. The passion of my heart became a cry to see the demonstration of the power and gifts of the Holy Spirit.

Since the time I began to read the Bible, I have had a great admiration for Saul of Tarsus—the apostle Paul, as he is more commonly known. He, too, was a hardheaded skeptic and a persecutor of the church. One of my favorite passages of Scripture is found in his first letter to the Corinthians:

> *My message and my preaching were not with wise and persuasive words, but with a demonstration of the Spirit's power; so that your faith might not rest on men's wisdom, but on God's power.* (1 Cor. 2:4–5)

That verse has become for me something of a personal mission statement. One of my greatest desires has been to see the marriage between the ministry of the Word and the demonstration of the power of the Holy Spirit. Having witnessed and participated in that very thing, only gave me a hunger for more powerful and consistent expressions of the gifts of the Spirit through every believer in the body of Christ.

THE INTENTIONS OF THIS BOOK

One of the most controversial topics throughout the church age has been the miraculous power of God and the gifts of the Spirit. The research conducted from both ends of the spectrum would fill countless library shelves. Church history scholars and theologians have wrestled with the ability of man to be an agent in the hands of God through which bona fide miracles occur.

This book is not intended to be an apology concerning the gifts of the Spirit. The church has spent far too much energy building doctrinal barriers that separate us from one another and, perhaps, even from the Holy Spirit. The goal of this book, then, is threefold.

A Reaffirmation of God's Plan

First of all, it will establish and reaffirm God's original intention to use spiritual gifts as a means of delivering, strengthening, and building up His people. It will illuminate God's concern for His people and the church to walk in victory. Experiencing abundant life through Jesus Christ is attainable; therefore, the words spoken by the apostle Paul are still echoing throughout the portals of glory: *"Since you are eager to have spiritual gifts, try to excel in gifts that build up the church"* (1 Cor. 14:12).

Demystification of God's Word

Secondly, in this book I will attempt to untangle the web of mysticism and complexity that has wrapped itself around the simple truth of God's Word. Most Christians have a tendency to think of the supernatural power of the Holy Spirit as something far removed from the normal course of everyday life or as something gained with great difficulty. They think such power is, for them, unattainable. If something is not easily grasped by sense knowledge, they quickly cry, "Impossible!" The term *sense knowledge* refers to information gained through the five senses (touching, hearing, seeing, smelling, and tasting).

My objective is to demystify the sensational and theological interpretation of the charismatic gifts so that a working knowledge can be grasped by the reader. To move in the spiritual gifts requires a proper mindset toward the gifts and a solid understanding of the intentions of the Holy Spirit. The desires of the triune God are not complex. The same hindrances that kept me from becoming a Christian are the same as those that keep people from moving in the power of the Holy Spirit.

Imagine that entering the realm of the power of the Holy Spirit were as simple as entering into true worship. "That's hard to believe," you may think. Indeed, worship is as much a supernatural act as entering the realm of the Spirit's power. Nevertheless, operating in the gifts of the Spirit is easy. If you can worship, you can also operate in the gifts of the Spirit.

Motivation for Greater Manifestations

Lastly, my goal is to motivate the believer who already operates in spiritual gifts to function at a higher order and greater diversity of manifestations. I do not claim to know all about the gifts of the Spirit; but, the knowledge that I do have, I want to use in building the kingdom of God. Paul, in his first letter to the Corinthian church, established the point that there are varieties of gifts, effects, and administrative levels of spiritual manifestations. (See 1 Corinthians 12:4–6.) Choosing to excel in these gifts is a personal choice. What motivates me to grow in deeper levels of spiritual manifestations is the image of Jesus, my Lord, as He hung on the cross dying for me—an image that is indelibly printed on my soul.

——Chapter 1——

Natural Enemies of Spiritual Gifts

—————*Chapter 1*—————

Natural Enemies of Spiritual Gifts

*The man without the Spirit does not accept the things
that come from the Spirit of God, for they are
foolishness to him, and he cannot understand them,
because they are spiritually discerned.
—1 Corinthians 2:14*

The terms *spiritual gifts* and *easy* are not often associated
with each other in the minds of Christians. Most people
think there is something very difficult about moving in
the power of God. Their impression of God is that of a reluctant
ruler—with people below Him, begging for a crumb or trying to
wrestle from Him something that they desperately need.

Jesus' parable of the persistent widow and the unjust judge
(Luke 18:1–8) is sometimes used to illustrate the opposite of
what Jesus intended. The widow pestered the judge until she
wore him out. Finally, he gave in and granted her legal protection. The point was that the Father, who is a righteous judge, is
not like that. Jesus concluded, *"Will not God bring about justice
for his chosen ones, who cry out to him day and night? Will he
keep putting them off? I tell you, he will see that they get justice,
and quickly"* (vv. 7–8).

This perception of a God who plays hard-to-get can have
two very different effects.

First of all, some people beg, plead, and cry out to God in prayer meetings to such an extent that it reminds you a little of the prophets of Baal on Mount Carmel. In this biblical account, pagan priests were trying to entice their idol to send fire down to consume the sacrifice (1 Kings 18). From morning until sundown, they cried out with loud voice, leaped around the altar, and did everything they could think of to get Baal to "move." The idea was that their determination and sacrifice would force Baal to answer.

All the while Elijah was on the sideline egging them on. *"'Shout louder!' he said. 'Surely he is a god! Perhaps he is deep in thought, or busy, or traveling. Maybe he is sleeping and must be awakened.'"* (v. 27). And with that, they regathered themselves and redoubled their efforts. Finally, they started cutting themselves with swords. Now that's real dedication!

On the other hand, having doused the altar's wood and sacrifice with water, Elijah prayed, and God consumed it with fire. All the people fell on their faces and said, *"The LORD—he is God! The LORD—he is God!"* (v. 39).

I've heard people pray as if they had more faith in God's reluctance than in His willingness. Answers to prayer are not the result of how hard we ask, as much as they are the result of the confidence with which we ask.

Secondly, a perception of a stingy God will cause others to simply throw in the spiritual towel. They do indeed love God, and perhaps they believe in the power of the Holy Spirit. However, they consider the required degree of faith, dedication, and personal righteousness to be far beyond them. They view themselves as just average, common Christians; so, for them, there's no use in trying. James wrote to the churches about enduring difficult situations, saying that God *"gives generously to all without finding fault"* (James 1:5).

If spiritual gifts are so easy, then why don't we see them manifested in and through more Christians? Let me illustrate how easy is often made hard. God's salvation and forgiveness are given as free gifts. You would imagine that free gifts are the ones most easily obtained. But think of all the monumental things people have done through the ages in an attempt to earn their salvation. Think of all the people who believe that forgiveness is impossible for them. The problem is not that the gift of righteousness is so hard to obtain. It is that people keep themselves separated from God because of their natural tendencies to make it hard. In other words, they try to gain their salvation by works. The very act of trying to earn their salvation only separates them further from God. Ironic, isn't it?

It is no harder for Christians to move in the gifts of the Holy Spirit than it is to receive the gift of salvation. The goal is not twisting the arm of a reluctant God to forgive us or to manifest His power through us. It is simply putting away the attitudes that isolate us from Him and accepting what He wants to do in and through us.

There are, however, several natural tendencies that isolate us from God's power and prevent the gifts from flowing through us with ease. Just as our efforts to earn the gift of salvation are an enemy of salvation, these tendencies that are common to all of us are generally the enemies of the supernatural powers of God and, in particular, the spiritual gifts of the Holy Spirit. Here, I present five of these enemies of the gifts of the Holy Spirit.

THE NUMBER ONE ENEMY OF SPIRITUAL GIFTS: FEAR OF THE SUPERNATURAL

Bertrand Russell once said, "Fear is the main source of superstition, and one of the main sources of cruelty."[1] The tendency of human nature is to avoid things that are mysterious or beyond rational explanation. For this reason, most Christians approach the subject of the supernatural with much trepidation. No one is afraid of a Bible study on the topic. But a personal challenge to be used by God in the realm of the supernatural would make most people very apprehensive. If you were to put them in an environment where the gifts are being demonstrated, it would make them very, very nervous.

The first time I witnessed the operation of the gifts of the Spirit, there was a noticeable uneasiness in my heart. I was invited to a large charismatic church by a Christian woman. As an unbeliever, I sat respectfully in my seat, thinking back through how I had been talked into coming, and I was determined not to repeat the mistake. It was an enthusiastic group, and back then I was unsure what everyone was so excited about. At one point, an elderly gray-haired man in the congregation stood up and loudly announced that God was going to heal a woman of cancer that very night.

I can't say I didn't believe that God could or even would heal a person of cancer. It's always easier, though, to believe something like that happening in another time and in a distant place. The idea of someone predicting that it would happen then and there—boy, did I feel uncomfortable! And how could this man say with such certainty, "The Lord would say to this people..."? I was looking for the nearest exit!

Despite all my personal reservations about this man's seemingly disruptive behavior, a frail woman walked up to the front of the sanctuary, announced she had cancer, and claimed that the prophecy was speaking about her condition. Some of the men, who appeared to be the leaders, prayed for her. The woman seemed to be powerfully affected by what was happening. She even stood up before the congregation and said that she felt the power of God healing her cancer and that all the pain was gone.

Though I witnessed a notable miracle, I kept telling myself, "Nothing happened to that woman. Those people at that church are just crazy." Several days after the service, my friend informed me that the woman had gone in for more tests. The doctor who performed the reexamination had proclaimed her free of cancer. Although I couldn't deny what I had seen, I surely didn't want to believe it, either. I desperately sought a rational explanation because the supernatural answer really scared me. It forced me to rethink my beliefs and the comfortable structures of logic I had erected in my mind.

Fear has both a positive and a negative side. Fear, in a positive sense, is the natural response to danger or pain (i.e., falling rocks, gunfire, etc.). The negative side of fear, which is based on ignorance and dread of the unknown or unfamiliar, creates superstition, prejudice, misinformation, and bad theology. Both types of fear are common to all people. But, as Christians, we cannot let our theology or our practical experiences be governed by our fear of the supernatural.

Natural Enemies of Spiritual Gifts

Terrified by the Things We Hold Dear

Christians believe in eternal life, in heaven and hell, in the resurrection of Jesus and His second coming, as well as the parting of the Red Sea, Elijah calling down fire from heaven, and a long list of other miracles. You would think that people who base their lives on such radical ideas about the supernatural would be drawn like magnets to the supernatural. But none of these biblical miracles makes us uncomfortable because they are conveniently removed far from our present experience, either in the past or the future. The truth is that most Christians are generally terrified of things they love, hope for, and believe.

God wants us to enthusiastically embrace the supernatural. The Scriptures are full of instances where angels, who appeared before men, first said to them, *"Do not be afraid"* (Dan. 10:12; Luke 1:13, 30; 2:10). Human beings are not used to dealing face-to-face with spirit beings. And angels, unlike the paintings of babies with wings, are scary beings! Because God knows and understands this fact, He ensures that all of His messengers quiet our palpitating hearts by saying in an extremely believable and reassuring way, *"Do not be afraid."*

Many times the Lord, in response to our prayers, sends His angels to fight on our behalf or to deliver messages, but it is in the form of a vision (Acts 10:1–8; 27:21–26). When our eyes are opened to their reality, those comforting words, *"Do not be afraid,"* need to be quickly heard.

Jesus cast a legion of demons out of a man who had terrorized all the people of the region with his demonically inspired, superhuman strength and animalistic behavior. This miracle was quickly reported to the townspeople, who came to see for themselves. The demoniac whom they had feared for so long was *"sitting there, dressed and in his right mind"* (Mark 5:15), talking to Jesus. You would suppose that they would have all rejoiced, saying with great joy, "Praise the Lord! We don't have to worry anymore about being attacked by the crazy man!" But that was not the case.

> *Then all the people of the region of the Gerasenes asked Jesus to leave them, because they were overcome with fear. So he got into the boat and left.* (Luke 8:37)

This was indeed a strange response, but one that is a common tendency of all natural men and women. It is also interesting to note that Jesus didn't hang around to do more miracles in a place where He was considered unwelcome by people who were squeamish about the power of God.

Matthew indicated that, when Jesus walked on the water, the disciples who were in the boat thought He was a ghost and were afraid. Once again, those comforting words were spoken: *"It is I. Don't be afraid"* (Matt. 14:27). Peter cried out in reply, *"Lord, if it's you...tell me to come to you on the water."* Jesus' response was, *"Come!"* (vv. 28–29).

This gospel narrative established the biblical premise that God does not want us to be afraid of supernatural things or spiritual gifts. He bids us to come and walk with Him in the miraculous. This is an eternal invitation for you and me to take a step of faith out of our comfort zones, amid our gawking friends, and dare to believe that God can use us to demonstrate His power.

Inordinate Fear of the Devil

Several years ago, I was in a worship service where the pastor began to pray for a man who was demon possessed. As the pastor commanded the demon spirits to come out, the man fell to the floor and began moving backward in a spiral form, like a snake slithering quickly away from its predator. I had never seen anything like that before. It was as though someone was pulling this man by the collar as fast as possible. The serpentine motion was very unusual, especially for a human being. The demonic spirits that possessed him were frightened and were trying with all their might to escape without being exorcised.

A Christian woman standing by became fearful in much the same way as did the townspeople in Gerasenes. Apparently, she had never witnessed an exorcism before. She swooped up her young son in her arms and ran to the back of the sanctuary, away from all the commotion. Her son showed no signs of any fear. The mother, however, was fearful for her son. Little did she know that God had already provided protection for her and her son through the covenant of salvation. The pastor cast out the demon, and no one was hurt, not even the frightened lady or her son.

Some reject the manifestations of the power of the Holy Spirit because they are so afraid of the Devil. The idea is that, since some manifestation might possibly be of the Devil, they will therefore have nothing to do with any kind of supernatural manifestation—just to be safe.

If God had not already protected us, there is nothing the woman could have done in her own strength against Satan. Running to the back of the sanctuary, or out of the building and down the street for that matter, has no protective ability against the attack of a demonic spirit. But we have no reason to be afraid of spirits, the unseen world, or supernatural gifts. God has everything under control. John the apostle wrote, *"You, dear children, are from God and have overcome them, because the one who is in you is greater than the one who is in the world"* (1 John 4:4).

There is a simple statement made by pastors in a lot of local churches which causes a common response from their congregations. The pastors say, "God is good," and the people respond, "All the time." As simple as this sounds, it is, nonetheless, very biblical. For a more scriptural phraseology, the psalmist put it this way: *"Give thanks to the LORD, for he is good"* (Ps. 136:1). Throughout the Bible, it is clear that God is good, and all things that come from His hands share that same quality of state. The gifts of the Spirit are good. They have been given to the church as tools to build up the body of Christ (1 Cor. 14:4–5, 12).

In fact, the apostle Paul established the premise by which we should pray to receive spiritual gifts: *"Since you are eager to have spiritual gifts, try to excel in gifts that build up the church"* (1 Cor. 14:12). The care for the church body should be the motivation for inquiring about spiritual gifts. And the main reason why someone cares for another person is that he seeks the person's good. The more you care for people, the more God wants to use you. The Lord really is our Shepherd who provides for our needs. It is with this intention that God gave us spiritual gifts.

I've met some Christians who are afraid to ask for the gifts of the Spirit or to step out in faith to be used by the Holy Spirit in a supernatural way. They are afraid that what they receive might be from the Devil. But read what Jesus said:

> *So I say to you: Ask and it will be given to you; seek and you will find; knock and the door will be opened to you. For everyone who asks receives; he who seeks finds; and to him who knocks, the door will be opened. Which of you fathers, if your son asks for a fish, will give him a snake instead? Or if he asks for an egg, will give him a scorpion? If you then, though you are evil, know how to give good gifts to your children, how much more will your Father in heaven give the Holy Spirit to those who ask him!* (Luke 11:9–13)

This is rather conclusive: God wants to give us our heart's desires. All we need to do is ask. If you have asked already and have not received a genuine manifestation, it is important that you continue asking. The words *ask, seek,* and *knock* are all in the present imperative, a tense that signifies continuing action. These words can also be literally translated, "continually ask, continually seek, and continually knock." According to *The Interpreter's Bible,* this means that Jesus is urging us to keep on asking, keep on seeking, and keep on knocking continuously, uninterruptedly.[2] These actions demonstrate the urgent sincerity we ought to regularly exercise.

Norval Geldenhuys, a New Testament scholar, comments on these three verbs by pointing out that we must ask, seek, and knock with "all other exertion…towards the purpose of obtaining the things for which the prayer is offered. While confidently awaiting God's answer, the one who prays must also from his side do everything that is necessary."[3]

Jesus concluded His statement to the disciples by affirming that, if earthly fathers desire to give good gifts to their children, how much more does our heavenly Father want to bless us (v. 13). This point negates any false thinking or fear that tries to enter the heart of the Christian who desires the manifestation of spiritual gifts. Whatever comes from God is good—including spiritual gifts. In fact, these gifts are innately good. That is why Paul said, *"No one who is speaking by the Spirit of God says, 'Jesus be cursed,' and no one can say, 'Jesus is Lord,' except by the Holy Spirit"* (1 Cor. 12:3). The Spirit of God will never cause anyone to operate in spiritual gifts via demonic influence. If one is not careful, however, fear of spiritual gifts can result in one unknowingly creating an enemy to the activation of spiritual gifts.

THE SECOND ENEMY OF SPIRITUAL GIFTS: SOCIAL ACCEPTANCE

Throughout church history, the gifts of the Spirit have been avoided by well-intentioned saints who were unable to detect the invisible war between social acceptance and the supernatural.

I grew up in a household that took pride in being socially intelligent. This became a significant part of my culture. One Sunday morning the Lord told me to visit a particular church in another city to deliver a prophetic word. I did not know the pastor but had heard a little about him from mutual friends. On Sunday morning I arrived to join them for worship, but the only empty seat was located directly against a wall, approximately six or seven seats from the nearest aisle.

As the worship time was coming to a close and everyone was still standing, a prophetic word came to me. I knew by its internal intensity that demonstrative gestures should accompany the spoken word. Since everyone was standing during worship, the quickest way to get to the nearest aisle was to walk over the six or seven chairs next to me. So I jumped up on the chairs and began to make my way to the aisle. I walked around waving my hands like one of the Old Testament prophets who would have been labeled a madman. I was prophesying loudly that the church had to be willing to release the pastor to the nations so that he could fulfill his translocal calling.

The prophetic delivery was so intense that the worship leader did not know what to do or say afterward. The pastor walked forward to the platform and said in the microphone that he did not know who I was, but it was indeed a true word from the Lord.

If that church or I were more caught up with external dignity, the word of the Lord would not have been given or received. Although my culturally preferred behavior pattern was opposed to that style of prophetic delivery, obedience to the word of the Lord is more important than social acceptance. Today, that pastor has a powerful international ministry based out of that same local church I visited. The church graciously received the word and acted upon it.

For Crying Out Loud!

When it comes to socially approved religious etiquette, there's just no place for crying out with a loud voice. God sent a prophet to King Jeroboam, who had set up his own altar so that people would not go up to Jerusalem in obedience to God's command.

> *By the word of the LORD a man of God came from Judah to Bethel, as Jeroboam was standing by the altar to make an offering. He cried out against the altar by the word of the LORD: "O altar, altar! This is what the LORD says...."*
> *(1 Kings 13:1–2)*

Mary, the mother of Jesus, went to visit Elizabeth, the mother of John the Baptist, when they were both pregnant.

> *At that time Mary got ready and hurried to a town in the hill country of Judea, where she entered Zechariah's home and greeted Elizabeth. When Elizabeth heard Mary's greeting, the baby leaped in her womb, and Elizabeth was filled with the Holy Spirit. In a loud voice she exclaimed: "Blessed are you among women, and blessed is the child you will bear!"*
> *(Luke 1:39–42)*

Mary had already entered Elizabeth's house. Nevertheless, the Bible declares that Elizabeth cried out with a loud voice while delivering a prophetic word.

Neither disrupting a worship service with a word for the king who is in attendance nor yelling out in someone's home are socially acceptable forms of behavior. Yet, it was God who orchestrated both of these instances.

People in the Bible often cried out loudly to prophesy or to ask for a miracle by faith. When Solomon dedicated the temple in Jerusalem, when Elijah prayed for the son of the widow of

Zarephath to be resurrected from the dead, when Isaiah the prophet cried unto the Lord and God brought the shadow ten degrees backward, when Jesus commanded Lazarus to come out of the grave, and when Stephen was being stoned to death while asking for his murderers' forgiveness—they all had one thing in common. They cried out with a loud voice. Throughout the book of Revelation, angels and cherubim and the heavenly host cry out with a loud voice, without ceasing!

The social pressure can become so overbearing that well-intentioned believers gradually slip into a pseudo-spiritual, non-supernatural Christian worship and lifestyle. For example, the presentation of a sermon in a teaching format is more "religiously correct" than a fiery preaching style. A hymn that is sung like a funeral dirge is more socially acceptable than an exuberant charismatic chorus. Religion that is approved by the world is not supposed to move one to external expressions of enthusiasm or excitement. Consequently, this type of environment makes many people think that a refined and dignified ministry (lacking a manifestation of spiritual gifts) is more honored by God because of its social grace and style.

THE THIRD ENEMY OF SPIRITUAL GIFTS: THE CARNAL MIND

Granted, the supernatural is not easily understood by the carnal mind. The term *carnal* refers to the natural, unregenerate way of thinking, not necessarily to something morally evil. The spirit realm calls for faith and an acceptance of God's unfailing ability to do exceedingly abundantly above all we could imagine or think. The logic of the Holy Spirit and how He manifests Himself in the church through the gifts is not according to our way of thinking or reasoning. His ways are higher than our ways, and His thoughts are higher than our thoughts (Isa. 55:9).

Every few months there is a cover story in *Time, Newsweek,* or *U.S. News & World Report* about miracles, the Resurrection, or the true identity of Jesus. In short, all these magazines simply rehash old arguments about controversies that exist between historic Christianity and the philosophy of the modern world. What complicates the matter is that the battle lines are not so clearly drawn, primarily due to the fact that over the centuries a lot of the world's materialistic philosophy has wormed its way into Christian theology.

Now, you need to understand that materialism is the philosophical belief that the material world as seen by the five senses is the fullness of the universe and that the spiritual realm does not exist or is not significant. As a consequence of this philosophy working its way into theology, the church has for a long time been at odds with itself over the philosophical foundation of faith. Some of the implications are very subtle. On the other hand, the best and most telling indicator of the foundation of faith is in the way one approaches the subject of miracles and, in particular, spiritual gifts.

For a thousand years, Christian theology was based on a worldview similar to the philosophy espoused by Plato, namely, that the most real things are unseen and that what is seen is created by the unseen. For Christians, that would be the spiritual world. Beginning around the twelfth century, there was in the Western World a great renewal of interest in classical literature. Both Plato and Aristotle believed that truth is only gained through reason. However, Aristotle disagreed with his teacher, Plato, and said that the only reality is in the material world. Donald Palmer, in his book, *Looking at Philosophy,* says that the rationalism and materialism of Aristotle were becoming so universally accepted that they threatened to bulldoze the Christian faith.[4]

The church eventually adopted the position found in the writings of Thomas Aquinas, who incorporated Aristotelian materialism into Christian theology by separating the spiritual world and the physical world. Aquinas considered the spiritual world to be governed by the spirit, and the world in which we live by rationalism–materialism. According to William DeArteaga in *Quenching the Spirit,* it was an effective answer to the Aristotelian skeptics, but there was little room left for the miraculous in this world.[5]

Many people who stop believing in God's involvement in the world through the miraculous eventually stop believing in the supernatural altogether. A recent poll of American Christians by the renowned marketing analyst, George Barna, indicated that, when asked the question, "Do you believe in the reality of Satan?" fifty-one percent of the twelve hundred Christians polled said that they did not know or that Satan was only a symbol of evil.[6]

The result of such a materialist worldview can take two religious forms. The first is cessationism, which is based on philosophical skepticism (there is no God or supernatural). The other religious form is based on theological skepticism, which is a religious attempt to argue against the presence or possibility of the miraculous. Those who take on the latter form are called demythologizers.

The Cessationists

Jack Deere, in *Surprised by the Power of the Spirit,* says that cessationism is the belief that all miracles and all gifts of the Spirit ended with the death of the apostles.[7] This belief is not based on Scripture itself but is an attempt to explain the absence of the power of the Spirit in the church. Augustine, in his early life, was a cessationist, but he completely reversed his position because of the number and frequency of miracles he witnessed in the fourth century church.[8]

Many conservative, fundamentalist Christians are dogmatic cessationists. Undoubtedly, they believe that the world of the Spirit exists but that the spiritual realm, in the form of miracles and the spiritual gifts, never affects the world we live in. You might call it a sort of "materialistic interlude" between the early church and the second coming of Christ. If it appears that a miracle has occurred, the automatic conclusion is either that it did not happen or that the Devil did it, because, of course, miracles do not happen in the church age.

The Demythologizers

Early in the twentieth century, skeptical theologians (most notably, Rudolf Bultmann) took the next logical step of cessationism: not only do miracles not take place today, but they never did.[9] The assumption was that the miracles of the Bible did not actually occur because it is not possible that miracles can occur. From this assumption, the task became to "de-myth" the Bible by giving rational explanations for all recorded miracles.

Consequently, according to *Eerdman's Handbook to the History of Christianity*, the Virgin Birth, the Resurrection, the miracles of Jesus, and so on, are all considered legends created by the early church.[10] The result is a materialistic belief system that is non-Christian because it is stripped of all the essential elements of faith. Unfortunately, the ideas of Bultmann and other demythologizers are taught in most denominational seminaries. No wonder the church is so powerless!

When you try to incorporate the philosophy of the world into Christian theology, you always end up with logical inconsistencies. Both the fundamentalist cessationists and the demythologizers are guilty of circular reasoning, a logical fallacy characterized by simply using a desired conclusion as the premise. In other words, as C. S. Lewis wrote in his book, *Miracles,* they reason in a circle by asserting that miracles do not happen because they cannot happen.[11] This kind of inbred theological skepticism about the miraculous, which is nothing more than a dogmatic commitment to doubt and unbelief, is an enemy of the gifts of the Spirit. Jesus Himself said that in His hometown He could only do a few miracles because of their unbelief (Matt. 13:58). Thus, the carnal mind, even when infused with biblical terminology, is a natural enemy to the supernatural.

THE FOURTH ENEMY OF SPIRITUAL GIFTS: THE DESIRE FOR CONTROL

The desire to control the form of worship and the way faith is practiced causes some people to make terrible mistakes in spiritual discernment and in the theology they concoct to support their faulty perceptions. Case in point: the Pharisees.

The word *Pharisee* means "separated one." The members of this Jewish sect prided themselves in having separated themselves from the clutches of worldliness. Being a Pharisee also meant that you spent most of your life studying Moses and the prophets. But, with all their devotion, they became theological hairsplitters who spent endless hours arguing over relatively insignificant points of the Law. This was, in their minds, what it meant to be truly spiritual. They took pride in being able to interpret the Law in such a way that it provided a prescription and a regulation for absolutely everything. All the questions were answered, and religion was fit into a neat little package.

Some contemporary theology is not so different from that of the Pharisees. Some modern-day Christians have determined that the Bible relegates all demonstrations of the power of the Holy Spirit to the Old Testament, to the first century church, and perhaps to heaven or the Millennium—but nothing to the present age. What's left are creeds, laws, and practices, in written or unwritten form, that work with or without the presence of God's power. In fact, the whole business of church, for them, could go on very well without any involvement whatsoever from God. That's not too exciting. However, it's very safe and very easy to control. That's what the Pharisees and their legal experts, the scribes, had created—predictable and manageable religion.

With all the accumulation of religious education and supposed ongoing communion with God, the Pharisees still lacked the basic knowledge of spiritual things. Consequently, the supernatural ministry of Jesus really caught them off guard. Jesus didn't have certified theological training, He cared little for their interpretations of the Old Testament, and, most importantly, He wasn't one of them. They probably would have considered Him easy to be discredited had it not been for all those miracles!

Jesus cast a demon out of a man who had been blind and dumb, so that he could both see and hear. This astounding miracle caused the multitude to take the first steps toward believing in Jesus as their Messiah. But the Pharisees, who could not refute the miracle itself, said, *"It is only by Beelzebub, the prince of demons, that this fellow* [Jesus] *drives out demons"* (Matt. 12:24).

Jesus used a simple argument to help them see that He could not be demon possessed and, at the same time, deliver a man controlled by demons. He said to them,

Every kingdom divided against itself will be ruined, and every city or household divided against itself will not stand. If Satan

*drives out Satan, he is divided against himself. How then can
his kingdom stand?* *(Matt. 12:25–26)*

Those Pharisees who asserted that Jesus had cast out demons by Beelzebub, the ruler of the demons, seemed to be more
concerned about protecting their religious control than they
were about discerning what was truly of God or of Satan. Consequently, Jesus condemned their evaluation in the strongest
possible terms:

*He who is not with me is against me, and he who does not
gather with me scatters. And so I tell you, every sin and blasphemy will be forgiven men, but the blasphemy against the
Spirit will not be forgiven.* *(vv. 30–31)*

It goes without saying that we need to be careful about as-
cribing supernatural manifestations to the Devil that may, in
fact, be the work of the Holy Spirit. It is also important to note
that God does not condemn people for making a sincere mistake
in judgment. But, in this situation, the Pharisees were not so
concerned about the origin of the miracle, whether it be from
God or Satan, as they were about maintaining their grip on or-
ganized religion. The Pharisees knew that if God were to intervene directly with His people through the miraculous, then they
would lose control.

The Pharisees were outright enemies to Jesus. Most Christians, when reading the accounts of Jesus' interaction with the
Pharisees, silently root for Jesus to verbally stomp them. Consequently, our modern-day religious packaging of worship services is not easily connected to the Pharisees.

Yet, there is a real and true parallel here. Rigidity, inflexi-
bility, and hard-and-fast rules regarding the Spirit of God work
against the supernatural in our worship services. Our corporate
meetings must offer a genuine ease and latitude for the Holy
Spirit to do whatever He chooses at any given moment. I am
not suggesting that there should not be a clear order and
structure to our services; I am simply pointing to the environment in which spiritual gifts are most easily manifested—an
atmosphere of freedom. In chapter eight I will further discuss

how we can create the proper atmosphere for the operation of spiritual gifts.

The Holy Spirit's work is like a kite flying in the wind. Too much tension on the string by the one flying the kite will prohibit the kite from soaring to new levels or moving laterally in new directions. Local church leaders hold the reins of the service. Hence, they set the direction and purpose of the meeting. If they are inflexible or insensitive to the Holy Spirit, the manifestations of the Spirit are quenched. Paul admonished us to *"quench not the Spirit"* (1 Thess. 5:19 KJV). *Quench* is the Greek word *sbennumi* (pronounced sben'-noo-mee), which means "to extinguish, to go out." We are urged not to extinguish or to allow the works of the Spirit of God to go out.

THE FIFTH ENEMY OF SPIRITUAL GIFTS: THE LACK OF DISCERNMENT

While many in the church are rejecting the supernatural, the world is making a fortune promoting toxic spiritual experiences of one form or another. Television commercials flood the screen daily, advertising psychic advisors who can provide you with supposed divine guidance on relationships, a career, and even the lottery.

Although the Bible clearly states that we must not seek after witches, warlocks, or anyone involved in psychic phenomena (Lev. 19:31), the spiritually uninformed are mesmerized by the mystery of the spiritual realm. The reason why there are so many commercials is that so many people are responding. This demonic lure has resulted in the psychic industry in America grossing multiple millions of dollars annually. Many in the church respond to this phenomenon by digging in their nails, so to speak, and fortifying their stance against any kind of supernatural manifestations. That way, they make sure none of the bad stuff can get in.

However, the apostles took a very different approach. The early churches that existed outside of Palestine were in a world filled with pagan mysticism and every kind of occult practice imaginable. They were like some people today who are content to let almost anything happen as long as they don't miss what

God wants to do. Did the apostles recommend that they prohibit spiritual manifestations in the church? Not at all. Nor did they recommend simply letting anything take place unchallenged. John wrote, *"Dear friends, do not believe every spirit, but test the spirits to see whether they are from God, because many false prophets have gone out into the world"* (1 John 4:1). With regard to prophecies from those within the church, Paul wrote, *"Two or three prophets should speak, and the others should weigh carefully what is said"* (1 Cor. 14:29).

Throughout the New Testament, the apostolic admonition was not to quench the Spirit's manifestations, but to discern. Discerning of spirits, one of the gifts of the Holy Spirit (1 Cor. 12:10), has been given to the church to help protect her from unwanted intruders and faulty spiritual practices. And, natural discernment has been provided to the church by God to ensure our health and purity. The body of Christ must learn to exercise with great wisdom the discerning of spirits so that the true gifts can be allowed to flow freely. The alternative is to announce to the world that all we have is a religious form without power.

One way to destroy the horrible occult industry, with all of its lies and false hopes, is for the church to move in the miraculous power of God. People would no longer seek the false when the genuine is in full demonstration and readily accessible.

Whether out of fear, ignorance, or a carnal mindset, many misguided saints unconsciously reject the power of God. The enemies of the gifts of the Spirit can have many damaging effects: people become insensitive to God, develop false doctrines in order to avoid dealing with the reality of spiritual gifts, and even ascribe authentic works of the Holy Spirit to Satan. We must begin viewing the gifts of the Spirit as means by which God delivers and empowers His church to live victoriously. A faith perspective is the best weapon we have in the war against fear, doubt, and unbelief.

Dr. Billy Graham tells the story of an Eskimo fisherman who came to a certain village every Saturday. He always brought his dogs with him, one black and the other white. The dogs were trained to fight on command. One Saturday the white dog would win. The next Saturday the black dog would win. The Eskimo would take bets from the observers, but he always knew which dog would win. When asked to explain the phenomenon, he replied, "I feed one dog and starve the other. The one I feed always wins because he's stronger."[12]

God wants you to operate in the gifts of the Spirit with ease. If you feed your faith, the enemies of the gifts will be starved into submission.

————*Chapter 2*————

Sovereignty and God's Calling

——Chapter 2——

Sovereignty
and God's Calling

Yours, O LORD, is the greatness and the power and
the glory and the majesty and the splendor,
for everything in heaven and earth is yours.
Yours, O LORD, is the kingdom; you are exalted as
head over all. Wealth and honor come from you;
you are the ruler of all things. In your hands are
strength and power to exalt and give strength to all.
—1 Chronicles 29:11–12

Jude, the half-brother of the Lord Jesus, wrote, *"Dear friends, although I was very eager to write to you about the salvation we share, I felt I had to write and urge you to contend for the faith that was once for all entrusted to the saints"* (Jude 1:3). Should Christians today seek and expect to walk in the power of the Holy Spirit in the same way the early church did? No question about it! Should they expect to actually see the same kinds of manifestations as did the early church fathers? Absolutely! We are charged by the apostles to earnestly contend for the faith that was delivered to the early church.

On the Day of Pentecost, when the promise of the Holy Spirit was initially poured out on about one hundred and twenty disciples, Peter stood up and said, *"The promise is for you and your children and for all who are far off—for all whom the Lord our God will call"* (Acts 2:39). The expressed intention of God was for the promise of the Holy Spirit to be given as a part of the inheritance that is common to all believers in every generation. Read the apostle Paul's exhortation:

> *I always thank God...for in him you have been enriched....Therefore you do not lack any spiritual gift as you eagerly wait for our Lord Jesus Christ to be revealed. He will keep you strong to the end.* (1 Cor. 1:4–5, 7–8)

Paul's understanding was that spiritual gifts were to continue without lacking to the very end. To put it another way, Jesus Christ will come again for a church that is operating in all the gifts of the Holy Spirit. Jesus Himself said that we would do greater works than He did because He was going to the Father (John 14:12).

The Christian faith was delivered once and for all to the saints through the apostolic witness. Jude wrote about the *"salvation we share"* (Jude 1:3) with those who received it at the very beginning. It was never intended that there should be one faith for the early church and another stripped-down edition for the generations that followed who are waiting for the revelation of our Lord Jesus.

The Greek word *epagonizomai,* which is translated into the word *contend* in verse three of Jude's epistle, is formed by two words. *Epi* is a directional word meaning "toward, upon, over." *Agonizomai* is the Greek word from which we get the English word *agony,* and it literally means "a contest."[1] The exhortation of Jude is to struggle, labor fervently, and fight earnestly to capture the faith that was delivered once by the apostles and is the same for all the saints.

The historical Christian faith delivered to us was established and built upon the supernatural acts of the Holy Spirit. To see the supernatural in operation in our lives and in the life of the church as it was at the beginning, is part of the great prize we seek to obtain. We don't need to compromise, theologize, or rationalize about it. We are exhorted by Peter, Jude, Paul, and all the early apostles to contend for it. From my eternal place in heaven I want to be able to reflect back on my earthly life and say, "I was not a spectator. I fought the good fight for the historic faith." In the words of many boxing greats, "I was a *conten-da!*"

The apostle Paul commonly used athletic imagery when he reflected on his own life or wanted to provide his readers with a word picture. In one of his letters he wrote, *"I have fought the good fight, I have finished the race, I have kept the faith"* (2 Tim. 4:7). To the Corinthians he wrote,

> *Do you not know that in a race all the runners run, but only one gets the prize? Run in such a way as to get the prize....Therefore I do not run like a man running aimlessly; I do not fight like a man beating the air.* (1 Cor. 9:24, 26)

The goal is not only to contend for the faith delivered to the early church, but also to actually attain it. Using Paul's analogy, we're not just running to run or throwing punches to stir up the air. The object of the race is to win, and the punch is no good unless it finds the target. So, if we really want to contend for the prize, we need to do it wisely and accurately.

Paul said in his second letter to Timothy, *"If anyone competes as an athlete, he does not receive the victor's crown unless he competes according to the rules"* (2 Tim. 2:5). When it comes to contending for the calling of God and the gifts of the Holy Spirit in the church and in your life, I know of two "rules" that must be understood: the sovereignty of God, and the grace of God. Appealing to and relying upon God's sovereignty and grace are like boxing with a left jab and a right hook. Winning the prize depends on knowing when and how to use each punch.

Unfortunately, some people appeal to and rely on the grace of God when they should be surrendering to His sovereign will and waiting patiently for His direction. Others are waiting for God's sovereignty to appear when, in fact, nothing will happen until they accept and act on the grace that is already provided. To contend for the faith of the early church, you must understand to which aspects sovereignty applies and to which aspects grace applies.

Grace and sovereignty are the key elements in the formulation of a theological framework in which the gifts of the Spirit are understood, handled, and activated. If we do not clearly understand this, the information may cause confusion and ultimately result in an inability to reconcile the lack of manifestations in the church today with God's desire to use us in the supernatural.

God, in His infinite wisdom, chooses to co-labor with man in the manifestation of spiritual gifts. This is in contrast to a sovereign move of God, in which He acts alone without the cooperation of anyone. Nothing that one does, says, or feels can either qualify or disqualify him to participate with one who acts sovereignly. Paul's statement to the Corinthian church shows clearly that we co-labor with God in manifesting spiritual gifts: *"Since you are eager to have spiritual gifts, try to excel in gifts that build up the church"* (1 Cor. 14:12). If manifestations of charismatic gifts were acts of sovereignty, Paul would not have counseled us to try to excel in the gifts—because we would have no part in their operation!

Let's look at the sovereignty of God and how we are blessed by it. Then, in chapter three, we will look at the dynamics of the grace of God.

SOVEREIGNTY IS HOW YOU LOOK AT IT

Why is it that two people can look at the same object or occurrence and walk away with two completely different points of view? Perhaps it's not *what* they see, but *how* they see. If this is true in the physical realm, how much more true this is concerning the things of the spirit and the realities of the unseen world!

We filter our perceptions through subtle, but very real, presuppositions and assumptions about God. Let me give you an example of how perceptions are affected by initial assumptions. A shoe manufacturing company in the United States sent two salesmen to the outback area of Australia to try to drum up some business. After several weeks one salesman wired back to the States and said, "Business here is lousy. The natives don't wear shoes." The following day the second salesman sent his update saying, "Business here is great. The natives don't wear shoes."

Why did these two salesmen have such different results? Simply, their perspectives were different.

Your perceptions about God, which have been shaped by your theological understanding of His ways, actions, and operations, may prove to be your biggest stumbling block or your greatest asset. Your view of sovereignty, grace, and your part in spiritual initiatives has a lot to do with whether you are a participant or a spectator in the manifestations of the Spirit.

A Bible teacher of mine used to share a story that shows how our understanding of eternal things is limited by our perceptions. Imagine the entirety of the human race marching down a road that ends at the edge of a cliff. People have been marching down the road and off the cliff for centuries. The only chance for escape is an exit ramp called Salvation that leads to a great door. It is the doorway to the kingdom of God.

Though many are called out and invited into the kingdom, most just continue on along their way to destruction. Those who choose wisely and turn aside are permitted to enter the kingdom through a great door, over which are written the words, *Whosoever will may come.*

Those who are turned aside are probably convinced of how wise they were to have made the right choice. Shortly after they have entered into the kingdom of God, they turn back and see the sign over the inside of the door which reads, *Chosen from the foundation of the world.* Both door signs are true, and both express realities about the nature of God. But how you understand either depends on your point of view.

WHAT THE BIBLE SAYS ABOUT SOVEREIGNTY

As Greek scholar Arthur Pink observes in *The Sovereignty of God,* the doctrine of sovereignty is "the foundation of Christian theology...the center of gravity in the system of Christian truth—the sun around which all the lesser orbs are grouped."[2] Consequently, what we believe about sovereignty affects every element of what we believe about religion in general. It also affects how we practice (or don't practice) those beliefs, including beliefs about the gifts of the Spirit.

The underlying theme throughout all of Scripture is that God is the Sovereign Creator, Ruler, and Sustainer of all things. *Sovereign* is an old Latin word that means "above all in authority and power." *Unger's Bible Dictionary* defines the sovereignty of God as "a term by which is expressed the supreme rulership of God. This is rightly held to be, not an attribute of God, but a prerogative based upon the perfection of the Divine Being."[3] The word also means "self-government; independent, supreme in authority and power." God who is sovereign has complete autonomy and power to function, regardless of what anyone else thinks, acts, or feels. He needs no one to get His desires approved or accomplished.

The doctrine of sovereignty is a significant one in the Bible and features a plethora of blessings. However, when we don't understand the role it plays in our perspective, then we fail to see God's power demonstrated through us. If we don't recognize the function of God's sovereignty in our contention for the supernatural manifestations of the Holy Spirit featured in historical Christianity, we will not be involved in these occurrences. It is not that God is unable to carry these things out Himself; it is simply that He has structured spiritual gifts to operate via a format other than sovereignty. What follows is an outline of a few of the major roles, provisions, and benefits that God's sovereignty has in our lives.

God Is Sovereign over All Creation

God announces to His creation,

For the LORD is the great God, the great King above all gods. In his hand are the depths of the earth, and the mountain peaks belong to him. The sea is his, for he made it, and his hands formed the dry land. (Ps. 95:3–5)

God is the Creator of everything that is. Think about that for a moment. Before the Creation, there was no matter and no space. The physical realm that we call the universe did not exist. There was only God and the spiritual realm. God created the universe through the Son, the *logos* or speech of God, by simply speaking forth His will (Gen. 1; John 1:1–3; Col. 1:16; Heb. 11:3). He also sustains and holds it all together by His very will, that is, by the *"word of his power"* (Heb. 1:3 KJV). As surely as God sustains everything by His word, He is intimately involved in our lives and in everything around us.

One day the heavens and earth will pass away (2 Pet. 3:10), right on cue according to His plan. Remember, the universe is not here on its own, as if it created itself. And it wasn't created by God because He had nothing else to do. It was created for a specific purpose, and when God's plan for it is accomplished, it will pass away.

God Is Sovereign over an Individual's Destiny

O LORD, you have searched me and you know me. You know when I sit and when I rise; you perceive my thoughts from afar. You...are familiar with all my ways. Before a word is on my tongue you know it completely, O LORD. You hem me in— behind and before; you have laid your hand upon me. Such knowledge is too wonderful for me, too lofty for me to attain.

Where can I go from your Spirit? Where can I flee from your presence? If I go up to the heavens, you are there; if I make my bed in the depths, you are there. If I rise on the wings of the dawn, if I settle on the far side of the sea, even there your hand will guide me, your right hand will hold me fast....

Your eyes saw my unformed body. All the days ordained for me were written in your book before one of them came to be
(Ps. 139:1–10, 16)

There are four blessings of God's sovereignty over a person's destiny that I want to mention. First of all, He knows us and has a plan for our lives long before we ever have any knowledge of Him or any desire to seek Him. When people have run as far as they can from God's presence, the Scriptures say that even there His hand will lead them (v. 10). How much more, then, will He lead those who seek with all their hearts to serve Him!

A second benefit of God's sovereignty is that our ultimate destiny cannot be modified by Satan. The rule of God functions as a guard, a protector, and a defender against anything or anyone that tries to thwart His plans. Satan must ask for permission when dealing with the heirs of salvation. (See Job 1:6–12.) In Luke's gospel, Jesus said, *"Simon, Simon, Satan has asked to sift you as wheat. But I have prayed for you, Simon, that your faith may not fail"* (Luke 22:31–32). What a great thing to know! God's sovereign reign makes us unconquerable to all foes. They can desire us, as Satan desired Peter, but to no avail. They can become even more aggressive like Satan, demanding permission. Nevertheless, God's sovereign plan will always prevail.

The real wonder of this benefit was realized when Jesus opened the heavenly veil to His disciples for a brief moment. Neither Peter nor the other apostles had known prior to this that Satan was in fact asking God's permission to separate Peter like chaff from wheat.

Not only is this example proof that our individual destinies are intact, it also leads to my third point, which is, the sovereignty of God increases our trust in the Lord. Peter did not understand at this time in his spiritual walk the existence of the doctrine of sovereignty, the doctrinal benefit of sovereignty, or the necessity of Jesus' prayer that his *"faith may not fail"* (v. 32). Peter was not even cognizant of his own heart attitudes, his propensity to cower under demonic attack, or how much he loved his own life. He would shortly be made very aware of all three.

Probably at the same time he was weeping about his third denial of Christ, Peter's trust in the Lord skyrocketed. Formerly, he had trusted his own strength, intellect, and leadership instincts. Now his security was in the fact that the Lord loves us in spite of our failures, past and future, and that He protects us in spite of our own weaknesses. Peter was beginning to grow in the trust that flows naturally out of the knowledge of God's sovereignty. The good news for us is that the Scriptures say the risen Lord Jesus Christ is at the right hand of the Father and *"always lives to intercede for* [the saints]" (Heb. 7:25).

Lastly, God's destiny for an individual cannot be defeated by other people, no matter how determined they are to thwart the purpose of God. Joseph's older brothers had conspired together to get rid of him. Yet God used their efforts to accomplish His purpose. Herod had imprisoned Peter and determined to have him executed because it pleased the Jews. If God has to send angels to intervene, which was the case in this situation, He will do so. No one can thwart the purpose of God working in a person's life.

Although this divine protection sounds great, over the years men have struggled with the doctrine of God's sovereignty. This is due in part to the fact that we all want to do our own thing, manage our own lives, and be our own bosses. James Boice says, in *Foundations of the Christian Faith,* "The basic reason why women and men do not like the doctrine of God's sovereignty is that they do not want a sovereign God. They wish to be autonomous. So they either deny God's existence entirely, deny this attribute of His existence, or else simply ignore Him for all practical purposes."[4]

God Is Sovereign over Our Circumstances

Amid all our trials, tests, and temptations, God still rules. Perhaps this is why Paul wrote, *"Rejoice in the Lord always. I will say it again: Rejoice!"* (Phil. 4:4). The phrase, *"Rejoice in the Lord,"* appears nine times in the Bible, and the word *rejoice* appears one hundred and ninety-two times in the King James Version. God means it! Rejoice, for He is in control!

"Yeah," you may think to yourself, "but what about all the problems I have?" From what we know about his personality, the apostle Peter had at one point probably asked the same question. Like all the apostles, Peter suffered many things for his faith in Christ. Toward the end of his life, when he was close to the time of his execution, he wrote the letter we know as First Peter. In it he made many references to trials and suffering.

> [You] *through faith are shielded by God's power until the coming of the salvation that is ready to be revealed in the last time. In this you greatly rejoice, though now for a little while you may have had to suffer grief in all kinds of trials.*
>
> *(1 Pet. 1:5–6)*

Peter continued to understand these difficulties in the context of God's sovereignty and protection—just as when he was almost sifted by Satan.

God Is Sovereign over His Own Grace and Mercy

Paul, in his letter to the Roman church, was dealing with the question, If Jesus was the Messiah, then why did the Jews reject Him? Paul's answer was that the calling of God is His sovereign choice.

> *What then shall we say? Is God unjust? Not at all! For he says to Moses, "I will have mercy on whom I have mercy, and I will have compassion on whom I have compassion." It does not, therefore, depend on man's desire or effort, but on God's mercy.* *(Rom. 9:14–16)*

When God calls a person to be used for a particular purpose, it is certainly not based on something that the person deserves or has earned. God's calling and choosing are only by His mercy. So, if, in order to accomplish His purpose, God desires to use one and not another, is He unjust to the vessel not used? Not at all, because there is no one who is deserving anyway. With God's sovereignty, there is no injustice associated with His decisions or actions (Ps. 19:9; 22:28). Everything He does is in accordance with His perfect justice, righteousness, and eternal plan.

It is also important to note that God rewards His servants, not according to how big or important their calling seems to be, but according to their faithfulness and obedience. Whether the task is large or small, their reward is according to their stewardship.

God Is Sovereign over History

David sang, *"For dominion belongs to the LORD and he rules over the nations"* (Ps. 22:28). Although we live in a fallen world, God still has things under control. David also wrote,

> *The kings of the earth take their stand and the rulers gather together against the LORD and against his Anointed*

Sovereignty and God's Calling

One....The One enthroned in heaven laughs; the Lord scoffs at them. *(Ps. 2:2, 4)*

Nebuchadnezzar, the king of Babylon, had a troubling vision that none of his wise men could interpret. But God revealed the vision to Daniel, foretelling that the king would be removed from power and would lose his mind for seven years. The reason for this was also declared to Daniel.

The decision is announced by messengers, the holy ones declare the verdict, so that the living may know that the Most High is sovereign over the kingdoms of men and gives them to anyone he wishes and sets over them the lowliest of men. *(Dan. 4:17)*

Military coups, civil wars, and influential national leaders (good or bad) do not, in themselves, determine the course of history. Regardless of free elections and the democratic process, leaders, good and bad, are raised up by God as a means of accomplishing His purpose. Bad leadership is one way in which God brings judgment upon a nation for its sin and rebellion.

During the interrogation scene that preceded Christ's crucifixion, Pilate said to Jesus,

"Do you refuse to speak to me?...Don't you realize I have power either to free you or to crucify you?" Jesus answered, "You would have no power over me if it were not given to you from above." *(John 19:10–11)*

Jesus made it clear to Pilate that his position of authority was solely the result of God's desire.

Perhaps history can be understood as a great play. The earth is the great stage, and the Father is the director. We know that there will be a glorious and happy ending, but how the drama works its way around to that ending is a great mystery. In every scene of every act there are all kinds of players who stand in the wings waiting to perform. Some, like Abraham, Saul of Tarsus, Martin Luther, or John Wesley, are brought forth in various scenes to say, *"The just shall live by faith!"* (Gal. 3:11 KJV). Great men like Moses, David, Abraham Lincoln, or Martin Luther King, Jr., are brought forth to center stage to lead with wisdom, courage, and integrity. But there are also the Judases, the Hitlers, and the Stalins.

He calls forth one to a place of prominence and gives another an insignificant part. When one is brought forth to center stage, he simply plays the part according to what is in his heart. Pharaoh who oppressed Israel, Nebuchadnezzar who sacked Jerusalem, Judas who betrayed Christ, and Pilate who condemned Him were only pawns in God's drama. Are they accountable for the wickedness of their hearts? You bet! But they gained their positions of authority and opportunity because God brought them forth to center stage to accomplish His will.

God Is Sovereign over Your Calling and Your Gifts

One good example of relying on a right hook (grace) when one should be thinking left jab (sovereignty) is the person who wants to possess a particular calling from God. You see, whether God has designed and purposed for you to be a prophet, a teacher, an administrator, or a counselor; whether He wants you to be gifted musically or athletically, it is an issue of His sovereign calling and purpose. It is not a matter of our initiative or of "claiming" a calling or an ability. When we relate to God on a matter of His sovereign plan and purpose, our response must be to surrender and obey. "Yes, Lord. Here I am; send me! Not my will but thine be done." That's how you must always respond to issues of God's sovereign will.

Regarding the callings and ministries in the church, Paul wrote,

> *It was he [God] who gave some to be apostles, some to be prophets, some to be evangelists, and some to be pastors and teachers, to prepare God's people for works of service, so that the body of Christ may be built up.* (Eph. 4:11–12)

It is important to note that an individual is not given the gift of the office of apostle, prophet, teacher, and so on. Rather, the person is the gift. God *"gave some* [people] *to be apostles...."* The person is the gift to the church, not the office to the person. The

48

calling of God makes you a gift to the local church, to nations, to the poor, or to whomever He calls you to serve—that is, if you are willing to say, "Yes, Lord."

At the same time, it is important to understand that, in order to be successful in what God sovereignly calls and gives you to do, you must be able to exercise the gifts of the Spirit He has given to you. While finding God's calling is a function of His sovereignty, exercising the gifts of the Holy Spirit that are given to you is a function of His grace. When we relate to God in a matter of grace, our response is to believe His word, accept His provision as a fact, and take the initiative to act on our faith in His promise.

Another way of thinking about it is this: By the sovereign purpose and plan of God, we become a gift. Our response to His sovereignty is to obey. On the other hand, by His grace He has freely given the Holy Spirit and the gifts of the Spirit. Our response to His grace is to receive the gift by faith and to step out upon that faith.

Unfortunately, some, in their efforts to contend for the faith delivered to the early saints, are trying to surrender to grace and receive sovereignty by faith—when, in fact, they should be surrendering to sovereignty and receiving grace by faith! They may be throwing a lot of punches, but for the most part, nothing is landing. As Paul would say, they are boxing *"like a man beating the air"* (1 Cor. 9:26).

—————Chapter 3—————

The Dynamics
of Grace

———*Chapter 3*———

The Dynamics
of Grace

*Each one should use whatever gift he has
received to serve others, faithfully administering
God's grace in its various forms.
—1 Peter 4:10*

W hat exactly is grace anyway, and what does it have to do with spiritual gifts? In the previous chapter I wrote about how to respond to God on issues that are governed by grace and issues that are governed by His sovereignty. It is important that we understand the difference.

Most Christians, playing a word association game, would immediately respond to the phrase *sovereignty of God* with what they consider its theological opposite, *the free will of man.* Sovereignty in opposition to free will, is so ingrained in our theological memory chips that when I say, "sovereignty verses grace," people do a mental double take and think to themselves, "Oh, he's substituting the word *grace* for *free will.*" You probably think that I've made a mistake, that I meant to write "free will" instead of "grace." But you read it correctly the first time: sovereignty versus grace.

You need to understand the difference between grace and sovereignty, and how it is that they are juxtaposed. For that matter, grace and free will are also on opposite sides of the so-called coin from each other. You see, whether it is the operation of God's sovereign will or of man's independent will, they are opposed to grace because grace does not work by itself. Grace is the mixing, the blending, the co-laboring of God with man. Grace is equated with neither sovereignty nor free will; it is God and man working and acting together as one.

How many times have you heard Christians lament over knowing when, on the one hand, to let go and let God have control or, on the other, to believe God and take a step of faith? Hang on, let go, step out, wait on the Lord—it can get pretty confusing. How do you let God do the work in the midst of your own working?

This is not an easy question, but it is nonetheless the goal of growing in grace. Growing in grace is learning to co-labor naturally with God. No one more than the apostle Paul struggled in his own efforts to serve God, only to fail completely. Yet the same man went on to accomplish more than any other apostle by learning to co-labor with God's grace. Read what he said about the secret of his success. It is an explanation that people who are still struggling with the co-laboring idea will find incomprehensible. Nevertheless, here it is:

> *But by the grace of God I am what I am, and his grace to me was not without effect. No, I worked harder than all of them— yet not I, but the grace of God that was with me. (1 Cor. 15:10)*

Grace is indeed, as it is so often defined, unmerited favor and forgiveness. But it is much more than that. It is also the power of God working through us, enabling us to do more and be more than we ever could in our own strength, wisdom, or ability. The nature of the Holy Spirit's gracious ability and gracious giftings is that they always work *with* us. As Paul said, it is *"by the grace of God."*

The development of the word *grace* from Greek classics to its use in the New Testament is very exciting. The Greek word for *grace* is *charis*. Prior to its use in the New Testament, *charis,* according to classical Greek, meant "a favor freely done, without claim or expectation of return." Greek scholar R. C. Trench states that, *"Charis*...is first of all that property in a thing which causes it to give joy to the hearers or beholders of it,...and then, seeing that to a Greek there was nothing so joy-inspiring as grace or beauty, it implied the presence of this."[1]

However, when *charis* was used by the writers of the New Testament to depict a flavor of God's character, the whole essence of the word changed. Trench adds,

> It is at that earlier point which we have just been fixing that *charis* waited for and obtained its highest consecration; not indeed to have its meaning changed, but to have that meaning ennobled, glorified, lifted up from the setting forth of an earthly to the setting forth of an heavenly benefit, from signifying the favor and grace and goodness of man to man, and thus, of necessity, of the worthy to the unworthy, of the holy to the sinful....Such was a meaning to which it had never raised itself before....[2]

THREE DYNAMICS

In the next chapter I will discuss how it is that we become co-laborers with God. But first, we need to think carefully about some of the dynamics of grace in our lives. The following are three of these dynamics of grace.

The Stumbling Block of Grace: It's Too Easy

Man's nature tries to find a way to ascend to forgiveness, to righteousness, or to God's favor by his own efforts. Everyone who believes in heaven is also naturally inclined to believe that his ticket is bought by good works. Paul said that the Gospel was a great stumbling block for the Jews, because righteousness was something they worked very hard at. How could such a great gift be given away on the basis of faith and not of works? It is absurd and contrary to the way "good, decent folks" think things ought to be.

But Paul wrote, *"For it is by grace you have been saved, through faith—and this not from yourselves, it is the gift of God—not by works, so that no one can boast"* (Eph. 2:8–9). You see, human nature always tries to tie the gift to some form of dedication or sacrifice that we make. But, no, it's only by grace, and grace is received only by faith. That's just too easy for some people to accept. Consequently, they stumble over grace.

There are two aspects of grace. One relates to mercy and the forgiveness of sin; the other refers to the power of God that enables us. The gifts of the Spirit are in the context of enabling grace. Neither aspect of grace is earned by our merits but is only received by faith. The gift of salvation and the enabling grace of spiritual gifts have both been provided. It is now up to those who are willing to believe and receive.

Grace Is Absolutely Free, but Very Expensive

According to *Nelson's Illustrated Bible Dictionary,* the word *grace* means "favor or kindness shown without regard to the worth or merit of the one who receives it and in spite of what that same person deserves."[3] God lavishly loves, protects, and uses us in a freehearted manner, irrespective of the fact that we could never merit this treatment.

It is important that we are always mindful of the fact that, though grace is given to us freely on the basis of faith, the gift is not cheap. It is free to us only because the enormous price of forgiveness was paid in full when the Son of God was offered as a perfect sacrifice.

Why doesn't God just grant universal forgiveness of sin so that everyone can go to heaven? The answer is that a God of perfect justice and holiness never overlooks sin or brushes it under the carpet, so to speak. You see, the greatness of God's justice and love are demonstrated, not in simply forgiving sin, but in *how* He forgives sin. Each act of forgiveness is made possible because its price is completely paid. Paul wrote to the Romans,

> *God presented him* [Jesus] *as a sacrifice of atonement, through faith in his blood. He did this to demonstrate his justice...at the present time, so as to be just and the one who justifies those who have faith in Jesus.* (Rom. 3:25–26)

The question is, How can God justify sinners and still remain just Himself? It is by paying for their justification with the blood sacrifice of Christ.

Every time I mention the word *grace,* be mindful of the fact that it is a pre-purchased grace, and it is for this reason that we can confidently expect to receive it.

Grace Is a Most Humbling Condition of Salvation

From man's perspective, sovereignty is quite humbling. Every knee buckles and bows to the awesomeness of God. James Boice says that once we accept the reality of God's sovereignty, "we find true freedom," and it "can become a wonderful doctrine from which we derive great blessings."[4] Sovereignty is humbling because it reminds us of who God is. Grace is humbling because it reminds us of who we are. Paul wrote that salvation is a gift, *"not by works, so that no one can boast"* (Eph. 2:9).

When a person comes to Christ by faith in His grace alone, he first has to quit trusting in everything else. You can't trust in Christ alone if you are trusting at the same time in your own works. It's either one or the other. Consequently, the person who comes by faith must first admit that all of his works, his own goodness, his own dedication, his own sacrifices, are worth nothing! Many people are just too proud and self-righteous to admit that.

> *Do you think Scripture says without reason that the spirit he caused to live in us envies intensely? But he gives us more grace. That is why Scripture says: "God opposes the proud but gives grace to the humble."* (James 4:5–6)

I assume that most people reading this book have had a salvation experience. Nevertheless, many may still need clarity on exactly where they are placing their faith. It's not faith in Jesus, plus good works, some church attendance, and a little tithing all mixed together that gains salvation for you. All those things are good to do, but it is faith alone in the grace of God purchased at Calvary. That's it—nothing more!

If you don't have a solid foundation of grace and faith in your life, everything you try to build on top of it will be a little off-center. Grace is the essence of co-laboring with God. Therefore, you cannot take hold of and apply co-laboring grace in all other areas of your life, including the manifestations of the gifts of the Holy Spirit, if you don't have a crystal clear understanding of pre-purchased grace that is received by faith.

SPIRITUAL MANIFESTATIONS BY SOVEREIGNTY OR GRACE?

When we consider the supernatural gifts, it is essential that we keep one thing in mind: the Bible teaches that the Holy Spirit assigns these gifts to each believer as He pleases (1 Cor. 12:11). This implies that the implanting of a gift in an individual's life is a sovereign act. God chooses what gift or gifts He wants you to have. You cannot alter that decision through prayer or fasting. That decision has already been made for you.

However, there is a big difference between being given a gift and exercising that gift. Just because God sovereignly gives you a gift doesn't mean that the gift will sovereignly exercise itself in your life, that is, manifest itself by God's will without your cooperation.

That is the whole point of Jesus' parable of the talents. We are the stewards of God's gifts. Look carefully at the comments of the apostle Peter: *"Each one should use whatever gift he has received to serve others, faithfully administering God's grace in its various forms"* (1 Pet. 4:10). Put simply, the distribution of gifts is based on God's sovereign will; the exercise or manifestation of the gifts is on the basis of co-laboring with the grace that is accessible to us by faith.

Gracious Deliverances

In 1 Corinthians 12:4, Paul stated, *"There are different kinds of gifts, but the same Spirit."* The word *gifts* is the Greek word *charisma*. The meaning of this word is "gracious deliverance." Therefore, this text could actually read, "There are different kinds of gracious deliverances, but the same Spirit."

With this illumination, the desires of the Father regarding the gifts of the Spirit are more clearly understood. God desires that His children experience some of the pleasures associated with eternal life here on earth. As a result, He provided the gifts of the Spirit as one means for us to receive "gracious deliverances" from the abounding problem of sin or from natural dilemmas and their effects on mortal man. Jesus Christ is the epitome of grace (John 1:16–17). Consequently, when we experience a manifestation of gracious deliverance, it really is a manifestation of Jesus' power and love for His people.

To grasp the operation of the gifts from a grace perspective, let's look at a biblical account involving Christ. There was a pool in Jerusalem around which all kinds of sick people would lie. The belief was that at a certain season an angel would come and stir the waters. Whoever was first into the pool would be healed. There was one man who had been there for thirty-eight years when he was approached by Jesus.

> He [Jesus] *asked him, "Do you want to get well?" "Sir," the invalid replied, "I have no one to help me into the pool when the water is stirred. While I am trying to get in, someone else goes down ahead of me." Then Jesus said to him, "Get up! Pick up your mat and walk." At once the man was cured; he picked up his mat and walked. The day on which this took place was a Sabbath.* (John 5:6–9)

Notice from the text that, prior to receiving his healing, the impotent man was waiting for a sovereign move of God, when an angel would come and trouble the water at a certain season. No one knew that season but the all-knowing, self-governing God.

Neither this man's spiritual condition nor those of the people waiting by the pool would play a role in determining who was to be healed. God came whenever He wanted and healed whoever jumped into the pool first. The fact that this man had suffered for thirty-eight years neither moved God nor gave the man the right to dive into the pool first.

However, little did the man realize on that day that grace was going to be present at Bethesda. Jesus, the fullness of grace, walked by and asked the man, *"Do you want to get well?"* (v. 6). In actuality, Jesus was asking the impotent man, "Do you want to receive a move of grace?" The man answered the question truthfully and received the manifestation of grace.

Three individuals are involved in a move of grace: God, the vessel through whom grace will flow, and the recipient of the ministry of grace. In this case, Jesus was the vessel through whom the grace of God flowed. The recipient of the gift of healing was the impotent man.

If the focus is only on God's sovereignty in regard to the gifts, this breeds irresponsibility on the part of the one who wants to operate in the gifts. Placing the sole responsibility upon God actually negates the involvement of both the vessel and the grace factor. It is our responsibility to take hold of the blessings of God, for *"the blessing of the LORD brings wealth, and he adds no* [sorrow] *to it"* (Prov. 10:22).

As the pastor of a local church, I challenge my congregation to learn to operate in the gifts through grace, not to wait for a sovereign move of God. I sometimes call upon those who exhibit a consecrated life, and say, "Give the word of the Lord to the congregation." If they tell me they don't feel led of the Spirit, I tell them, "I feel led. One of us is missing God, and I have a greater track record of accuracy."

This may seem very confrontational to you, and you're absolutely correct—it is highly confrontational. However, you must understand that a sovereign perspective on the gifts breeds lethargy and faithlessness in a believer's heart. As a shepherd, my goal is to create an atmosphere where grace can be manifested.

A church in which a large percentage of the members are sitting back waiting for some encounter with the gifts through contact with an awesome child of God clothed with sackcloth and covered with ashes is an unrealistic church. It rarely happens! The revelation needed in the church today is that each parishioner, each member of the body of Christ, is that awesome man or woman of God!

I remember in one of our church services I called upon a young prophetess to give a prophetic word to a man whom the Lord had instructed me to call forward. She looked at me with reservation and doubt in her eyes, then proceeded to lay her right hand upon the gentleman's forehead and pray. Immediately I stopped her and said, "I did not call upon you to pray a cute prayer. This brother is hurting, and he needs the word of the Lord spoken over his life."

When I challenged her to hear from God, she paused for a few moments and closed her eyes. Momentarily, a smile broke out on her face, and she began prophesying a powerful and accurate word describing the gentlemen's past and how God was going to bring him to a place of victory in the near future.

You may ask, "Why did all this occur?" Well, once the young prophetess was placed in a position where she had to hear from God, the grace factor came into play. Grace works through faith (Eph. 2:8)! The key, however, to seeing faith implemented is knowing how to have the perspective of grace.

Sovereign Prophesying

Undeniably, the gifts can be manifested by God's sovereignty if He chooses, but it is not the norm or the biblical teaching. Grace is the doorway to accessing and operating in spiritual gifts. When the gifts are manifested via sovereignty, it is an anomaly. One example, however, of the prophetic gift operating sovereignly occurred during the reign of Saul.

The king was threatened by David's presence and growing fame in the kingdom. Consequently, Saul relentlessly tried to kill his young rival, the one God had already anointed to be the next king. David had fled from Saul and had come to Samuel at Ramah. Saul eventually found out where David was and sent messengers to retrieve him. The account reads:

> So [Saul] *sent men to capture him. But when they saw a group of prophets prophesying, with Samuel standing there as their leader, the Spirit of God came upon Saul's men and they also prophesied. Saul was told about it, and he sent more men, and they prophesied too. Saul sent men a third time, and they also prophesied. Finally, he himself left for Ramah and went to the great cistern at Secu. And he asked, "Where are Samuel and David?" "Over in Naioth at Ramah," they said. So Saul went to Naioth at Ramah. But the Spirit of God came even upon him, and he walked along prophesying until he came to Naioth. He stripped off his robes and also prophesied in Samuel's*

presence. He lay that way all that day and night. This is why people say, "Is Saul also among the prophets?"

(1 Sam. 19:20–24)

Again, the word *sovereignty* means "complete independence and self-government." God used Saul and his messengers to prophesy in their murderous state of mind. They operated prophetically as a result of the sovereignty of God, irrespective of their own spirituality or their own will to cooperate or co-labor with the will of God.

This example characterizes the perspective many people have regarding the gifts of the Spirit. The average believer sitting in the pew on Sunday morning, of course, does not have murder on his mind. But he may be sitting there waiting for God to sovereignly cause a prophetic utterance to flow out of his mouth and edify the congregation. When the prophecy doesn't occur, the believer merely shrugs his shoulders and says to himself, "God didn't want to speak through me today, because, if He did, I would have prophesied." The same thing can be true for the other charismatic gifts.

The messengers of Saul prophesied, not only apart from their will and their faith, but probably against their will and their faith. But this is not the norm; it never was and, according to Scripture, it never will be. The ingredients of grace and faith are required.

The story of William Carey's missionary proposal is a more recent example of how people with a perspective locked in on God's sovereignty are unable to respond to God's grace. When Carey approached church leaders about a mission to India, their reply was, "If God wants to save India, He can do so without your help."

Carey, who commonly said, "Expect great things from God, and attempt great things for God," would not be discouraged. In 1792 he founded the Baptist Missionary Society, the first foreign missionary organization to emerge from the great English Evangelical Revival. Carey himself went to India and became one of the greatest and most successful missionaries of the Christian church.[5]

The apostle Paul said,

The Dynamics of Grace

How, then, can they call on the one they have not believed in? And how can they believe in the one of whom they have not heard? And how can they hear without someone preaching to them? And how can they preach unless they are sent?

(Rom. 10:14–15)

Could God have saved India without Carey, or someone like him? Certainly, He could have, but it is almost as certain that He would not have. God is looking for co-laborers.

As we have already learned from my references and biblical illustrations, the gifts of the Spirit can be manifested by God's sovereignty if He chooses. However, it is not the typical pattern. The ingredient of grace is required to unlock the supernatural exhibitions of the Spirit of God. I can't emphasize this enough.

Established within the Father's heart is His willingness to dispense grace to man in order to show him mercy. The Bible states, *"Let us then approach the throne of grace with confidence, so that we may receive mercy and find grace to help us in our time of need"* (Heb. 4:16). Grace ushers in mercy. It's the grace of God that releases the mercy of God during those times when we find ourselves in difficult circumstances.

Grace infers that God is willing to entertain the importunity of man. He reassures frail man that the throne of grace is approachable. "I will listen to your plea," says the Lord. Grace reflects God's humanity, and sovereignty reflects His divinity. Grace says, "Come to me at any time; I'll see what I can do right now."

This is exactly why many Greek scholars say that grace means "an act of spontaneous favor." The Father doesn't want to wait. It is as though His favor is a hot meal to a starving man, and, as soon as the man sits down at the table, the delicious meal is presented. On the other hand, it should be apparent to the believer that grace does not infer that God is man's servant, attempting to satisfy his every whim. Sovereignty says, "I choose to display My kindness at My prompting and not as a result of man's predicament, desires, or importunity." In essence, the sovereign God says to man, "The meal will be ready when I see fit, and not before then."

But sovereignty and grace are not at odds with each other. They are both necessary in our service unto God. Their roles and functions are just different. Hence, our expectations will be different once we realize how these doctrines impact us and are used in our contending for the faith once delivered to the church.

——Chapter 4——

Co-laboring
with Grace

——Chapter 4——

Co-laboring
with Grace

*How much more will those who receive God's
abundant provision of grace and of the gift
of righteousness reign in life through
the one man, Jesus Christ.*
—*Romans 5:17*

S alvation is not a sovereign act in and of itself, because man
must respond to God's calling and receive His precious
gift. How did you become a Christian, anyway? Did God do
the complete work all by Himself without any expression of
faith or obedience on your part? Did you have any input or a
say-so in the matter? Although the love of God is overwhelming,
it will not result in salvation without reciprocation and the full
cooperation of the individual.

That doesn't mean we have to perform a series of moral or
spiritual feats. God accepts us just as we are. For those who met
Jesus Christ in the flesh, as well as those who hear His Spirit
calling and convicting them, the response has to be, "Yes, Lord.
I believe, I repent, I will follow You."

There are those who err by leaning so hard on the aspect of
God's sovereignty that, for them, mankind's faith to receive or
willingness to obey is irrelevant. The reformed doctrine of
"irresistible grace" states that the human will is only an illusion.

In *A Dictionary of Christian Theology,* edited by Alan Richardson, the doctrine is put this way: God made you say yes to the Gospel; it had nothing to do with your choice or your faith.[1]

If, from your perspective, you see that God did all the work from beginning to end without your active participation, you lean far too heavily on the aspect of sovereignty. Do you remember when Jesus confronted Paul as he made his way to Damascus? As Paul lay on the ground, having dramatically perceived the calling of God, *"he trembling and astonished said, Lord, what wilt thou have me to do?"* (Acts 9:6 KJV). This same Paul wrote to the Romans,

> *For if, by the trespass of the one man, death reigned through that one man, how much more will those who receive God's abundant provision of grace and of the gift of righteousness reign in life through the one man, Jesus Christ.   (Rom. 5:17)*

The abundance of grace has been provided universally. However, its application and manifestation occur only in *"those who receive."*

Some emphasize man's free will to the point that it sounds as if they believe a person has the ability to be perfect by his own effort and willpower, apart from the empowering grace of God. Certainly, this is not the case. Others who take extreme positions on sovereignty believe in a limited atonement, that is, Jesus died only for a pre-chosen elect. Notwithstanding, the Scriptures say clearly that Jesus died for the sins of the world (John 3:16) and that He *"takes away the sin of the world"* (John 1:29). Why, then, are not all men saved? It is because the Scriptures also say, *"To all who received him, to those who believed in his name, he gave the right to become children of God"* (v. 12).

So then, the gift of salvation has been purchased and is made available to all those who believe and receive it by faith in Christ. In the same way, the grace and gifts of the Holy Spirit are readily accessible to those who believe and receive by faith. A solid understanding of how and why one receives the gift of salvation is the starting point for being a vessel through whom spiritual gifts operate.

As Paul lay there on the road, looking up into the light of truth, he quickly came to his senses and realized his responsibilities toward God. If our responsibilities have already become apparent to us regarding salvation, shouldn't we have a similar obligation with respect to flowing in the gifts?

The problem is that many believers have not yet realized that being *"the light of the world"* (Matt. 5:14) is not limited to sharing one's faith. It also includes demonstrating one's faith: *"Now to each one the manifestation of the* [Holy] *Spirit is given for the common good"* (1 Cor. 12:7).

Since the Holy Spirit is part of the Godhead, He is willing to manifest His presence and desires. Man cannot establish an expression of God without His input. Neither does God regularly exhibit Himself supernaturally in the earthly realm without man's input. God chooses to co-labor with redeemed man!

Scripture says, *"Surely the Sovereign LORD does nothing without revealing his plan to his servants the prophets"* (Amos 3:7). Now, man is not the one who decided that God must tell him everything He plans to do. God established this premise. I believe that one major reason why the Father chooses to co-labor with His sons and daughters is that He wants mature, responsible children.

When God considers establishing a friendship, He looks at the internal and external obedience of the candidate prior to any commitment. Because God wants genuine friends, He looks at the heart: *"the LORD seeth not as man seeth; for man looketh on the outward appearance, but the LORD looketh on the heart"* (1 Sam. 16:7 KJV).

When we look closely at the gifts, it is as though two friends are assisting each other for a mutual benefit. Man is working with God, and God is working with man for the express purpose of helping a third party experience a gracious deliverance. They co-labor because one of the advantages of the covenant is friendship. The friendship is so strong that they both want the same things.

Or, it is as though two buddies are traveling together in an automobile on a highway and both notice a woman in distress. Sometime before, the men had agreed that, in certain situations, it was mutually advantageous for them to work together.

This situation appears to be one of those times. The woman had accidentally driven her car over a nail and had a flat tire. Suddenly, the car in which the men are driving comes to a screeching halt, and both men simultaneously jump out to help the woman by changing her tire. They don't have to have a long-drawn-out discussion on the ethics of helping women with flat tires or what they should do. They already have a common understanding.

THE COVENANT AND CO-LABORING

Co-laboring is a covenantal issue. God's covenant with redeemed man includes the supernatural activities of the Holy Spirit. The actions and behavior of man stems from the value he places on God's promises that are intrinsic to the covenant. The word *covenant* signifies an agreement in which both parties bind themselves to fulfill certain specific demands and are guaranteed of receiving certain advantages. This foundation for co-laboring with God's grace is found in the covenant that God originally established with Abraham and extended to those who are the children of Abraham by faith (Rom. 4:16).

In Jewish history, when one ratified or sealed a covenant, an animal was normally sacrificed by cutting it directly in half. According to Ray R. Sutton in his book, *That You May Prosper,* "the sacrificial system was at the heart of covenant ratification. It expressed the need for atonement. It pointed to an oath that was made in terms of an object that took the place of man. It was directly linked to the covenant itself."[2]

One example of such a covenant is found in the book of Jeremiah:

> *The men who have violated my covenant and have not fulfilled the terms of the covenant they made before me, I will treat like the calf they cut in two and then walked between its pieces. The leaders of Judah and Jerusalem, the court officials, the priests and all the people of the land who walked between the pieces of the calf....* (Jer. 34:18–19)

After the sacrifice, the halves of the animal were placed opposite one another. One of the two parties would then walk through the halves and seal the covenant by burning the animal pieces with fire. By completing this act, the two parties were expressing to each other their continued commitment to fulfill all the specifications of the covenant, each aware of the impending curses that would fall upon the party who violated the agreement.

The familiar verse, *"May the* LORD *keep watch between you and me when we are away from each other"* (Gen. 31:49), is often used in Christian circles as some sort of benediction or blessing. Actually, the passage is a curse and a warning given by Laban to Jacob, in case he would consider reneging on his part of their agreement. It concludes, *"Even though no one is with us, remember that God is a witness between you and me"* (v. 50).

The term *cut a covenant* refers to this process. It is probably the origin of the modern term *cut a deal*. In Genesis 15, Abraham had a dream in which he saw a covenant being cut.

> *As the sun was setting, Abram fell into a deep sleep, and a thick and dreadful darkness came over him. Then the* LORD *said to him, "Know for certain that your descendants will be strangers in a country not their own, and they will be enslaved and mistreated four hundred years. But I will punish the nation they serve as slaves, and afterward they will come out with great possessions. You, however, will go to your fathers in peace and be buried at a good old age."...When the sun had set and darkness had fallen, a smoking firepot with a blazing torch appeared and passed between the pieces. On that day the* LORD *made a covenant with Abram.* (Gen. 15:12–15, 17–18)

It is interesting to note that Abraham did not pass between the pieces of the animals. He was only a spectator. The whole vision was symbolic of the fact that God had made a covenant with Himself. This is reflected later on when He says to Abram concerning the covenant, *"I swear by myself"* (Gen. 22:16).

Every covenant has conditions to be met and promises to be delivered. In this covenant, God made promises, and God, in the person of Jesus Christ, fulfilled the conditions. Consequently, Jesus received from the Father the full measure of the covenant promise. Someone once said that as Christians we have five thousand promises. Actually, the Bible says something very different. We actually have no promises.

The promises were spoken to Abraham and to his seed. The Scripture does not say "and to seeds," meaning many people, but "and to your seed," meaning one person, who is Christ.
(Gal. 3:16)

If Abraham and Christ were the only ones who received the promise, where do we come in? We become partakers of the covenant promise because, as it says in Romans, we are *"co-heirs with Christ"* (Rom. 8:17). The King James Version uses the term *"joint-heirs."* Why is this important with regard to the manifestations of the gifts of the Spirit? It is so for two reasons.

The Promised Inheritance Is the Gift of the Holy Spirit

First, the Holy Spirit and the manifestations of spiritual gifts were thought of by the apostles in terms of the promise of the covenant. On the Day of Pentecost, Peter stood up to explain the baptism of the Holy Spirit and the manifestation of the gift of tongues to the amazed onlookers. *"Exalted to the right hand of God, he has received from the Father the promised Holy Spirit and has poured out what you now see and hear"* (Acts 2:33).

Peter concluded his Pentecost sermon by saying, *"You will receive the gift of the Holy Spirit. The promise is for you and your children"* (vv. 38–39). In his letter to the Ephesians, Paul wrote, *"You were marked in him with a seal, the promised Holy Spirit, who is a deposit guaranteeing our inheritance"* (Eph. 1:13–14).

Co-heirs of the Promise Become Co-laborers of the Kingdom

Secondly, we become united, joined, and one with Christ by faith. That's what it means to be "in Christ." Think back to those five thousand promises. We receive the promises of God because we are joint-heirs in Christ. Read what the Bible says about the promises: *"For all the promises of God in him are yea, and in him Amen"* (2 Cor. 1:20 KJV). In ourselves, there are no promises. In Christ they are all yes and amen.

God's purpose has been to make us co-heirs of the promise in Christ. He made the provision, and we entered the covenant as we became joint-heirs by faith. That having taken place, His purpose is that we become co-laborers with the Holy Spirit, who has given spiritual gifts to all believers. But the gifts don't manifest themselves automatically or independently of us. It's neither the Spirit without us, nor us without the Spirit. It is a comingling, a meshing and a uniting of the Spirit's ability with our ability and availability—God's purpose working in and with our initiative. We are co-heirs with Christ to the covenant promise, co-laboring with the Holy Spirit to establish and advance the kingdom of God.

CO-LABORING RELATIONSHIP

Being a joint-heir of the covenant is a legal standing we have with God simply because of what Jesus Christ has done. Born-again Christians are joint-heirs, even though they may follow Him at a distance. It is through an ongoing relationship with God that we are able to move on and become actual co-laborers with the Holy Spirit through the manifestations of His gifts. The key to co-laboring is the relationship. Jesus said to His disciples,

> *If ye abide in me, and my words abide in you, ye shall ask what ye will, and it shall be done unto you....Ye are my friends, if ye do whatsoever I command you. Henceforth I call you not servants; for the servant knoweth not what his lord doeth: but I have called you friends; for all things that I have heard of my Father I have made known unto you.*
>
> *(John 15:7, 14–15 KJV)*

When we look closely at the gifts as they are demonstrated in the New Testament, it is as though two friends are assisting each other for a mutual benefit. Man is working with God, and God is working with man for the express purpose of helping a third party experience a gracious deliverance. They co-labor because one of the advantages of the covenant is friendship. Peter said to the lame man outside the temple, *"What I have I give you. In the name of Jesus Christ of Nazareth, walk"* (Acts 3:6). What confidence Peter had! Some might say is was presumptuous. How did he know it was God's will? The probable answer is that out of his relationship with the Holy Spirit, he simply had the same desires and the same agenda that the Spirit had.

Immediately following the prayer of faith, the lame man's feet and ankle bones received strength, and he began to walk. Notice that the manifestation of the gifts of healing occurred through the relationship Peter and John had with the Lord. The lame man received strength and healing because Peter, John, and God all had the same desire regarding the man. Notice also from the text that it was the hour of prayer (Acts 3:1).

How many believers who walked into the temple before Peter and John showed the slightest concern for the crippled man? Furthermore, how many of those self-professed "friends of God" inquired of the Lord's desire regarding the man? Doesn't redeemed man have a covenantal responsibility to make an inquiry into the desires and wishes of the One with whom he is in covenant? Absolutely!

Peter and John saw the man lying there in need of a gracious deliverance. The grace factor came into play, and they quickly discussed the idea with the Father. The Father agreed, and the gift of healing began to flow through them. God co-labored with His two friends, and the three of them solved the dilemma.

From this perspective of the gifts, the person(s) involved must realize that sovereignty does not co-labor; grace does. Sovereignty works well independently, but grace is relational; it needs a partner. When it comes to the gifts, grace somehow becomes more apparent in a covenant environment. Therefore, grace fosters the idea of a covenant; sovereignty generally does not.

Co-laboring in the Gift of Prophecy

I was asked for an interview by a young lady completing her masters degree in communications at Columbia University. She was working on a paper entitled, "Are There Modern-Day Prophets?" In the interview I asked if she had ever been prophesied to. She looked at me thoughtfully and finally said, "No, I have not." I then asked her permission to give her a prophecy.

After she had agreed to the request, I stood in front of her, laid my hand on her, and prophesied for about three minutes. Afterward she started shaking, being visibly moved by what she had heard. The Holy Spirit had given me clear and specific information about her life. She continued to shake for some time. Finally, she just said, "Amen!"

Not only did the Holy Spirit minister to her deeply through the word, but the experience helped her to understand and accept the validity of modern-day prophets. Before asking her if I could prophesy, I had no previous leading, no word from the Lord, no supernatural information at all, and no voice saying, "Prophesy over this woman." When you have a friendship with God, you find yourself wanting the same things that He wants and, therefore, flowing naturally in the gifts.

The gifts of the Spirit flow most freely out of a camaraderie with God. Jesus said that those who abide in Him would ask whatever they wished, because they were friends. When we get kingdom-oriented, seeking the kingdom first, then all things are given to us.

As I have already stated in this chapter, one major reason why the Father chooses to co-labor with His sons and daughters is that He wants mature, responsible children. The closer we get to Him, the more we find God's burdens and concerns becoming our burdens and concerns. In fact, we find God's concerns so evident that we pursue His longings as though they had been ours all along. It eventually becomes harder and harder to distinguish between God's motivation and our parallel motivation.

As we begin to sense the burden of the heart of God, we also begin to realize our own responsibilities. They become apparent to us regarding salvation when we by the Holy Spirit sense the depth of our sin, the love of God, and His sacrifice for us. As Paul lay on the road, he quickly realized his responsibilities toward God. *"Lord, what wilt thou have me to do?"* (Acts 9:6 KJV). Feeling God's heart for the church and for the world, don't we have a similar obligation to flow in the gifts?

Remember, being the light of the world includes demonstrating one's faith: *"Now to each one the manifestation of the Spirit is given for the common good"* (1 Cor. 12:7). The word *manifestation* means "a public showing, exhibition, and expression." Consequently, the text is saying that each of us has been given the public showing of the Holy Spirit. With this in mind, each time we attend church or tend to the affairs of the world, we do so with a responsibility realized from a close covenantal relationship with God.

Gehazi's Dilemma

When God co-labors with man, the camaraderie and oneness attributed to a covenant are greatly heightened. As a result, the gifts begin to flow out of the unity of purpose that the participants have.

One of the most dynamic prophets of the Old Testament was Elisha. The gracious deliverances in which God co-labored with him were born out of their personal friendship and covenant. One of the miracles performed by Elisha was the resurrection of the Shunammite woman's dead son (2 Kings 4:8–37). Just a few years before this notable miracle, Elisha had prophesied the birth of the boy, and now he was confronted with the frantic mother crying out for him to minister to her dead son.

We must realize that, prior to Elisha's ascension to the role of senior prophet, he was Elijah's servant. Elijah was training and mentoring Elisha. When he matured in his relationship with God, Elisha would receive the mantle of the prophetic ministry. All young prophets have visions and dreams of becoming greater prophets than their masters and mentors. With such a good role model, we are not surprised that Elisha would follow suit when he was the senior prophet. Indeed, when the Shunammite woman cried for his help, Elisha assigned the case to the young prophet he was mentoring, Gehazi, his servant (v. 29).

The very meaning of the name Gehazi is "valley of a visionary." Undoubtedly, this young prophet dreamed of one day surpassing his master in prophetic ministry. With this thought in mind, let us look closely at the passage of Scripture containing this incident.

> *Elisha said to Gehazi, "Tuck your cloak into your belt, take*
> *my staff in your hand and run. If you meet anyone, do not*

greet him, and if anyone greets you, do not answer. Lay my staff on the boy's face." But the child's mother said, "As surely as the LORD lives and as you live, I will not leave you." So he got up and followed her. Gehazi went on ahead and laid the staff on the boy's face, but there was no sound or response. So Gehazi went back to meet Elisha and told him, "The boy has not awakened." When Elisha reached the house, there was the boy lying dead on his couch. He went in, shut the door on the two of them and prayed to the LORD. Then he got on the bed and lay upon the boy, mouth to mouth, eyes to eyes, hands to hands. As he stretched himself out upon him, the boy's body grew warm. Elisha turned away and walked back and forth in the room and then got on the bed and stretched out upon him once more. The boy sneezed seven times and opened his eyes. Elisha summoned Gehazi and said, "Call the Shunam-mite." And he did. When she came, he said, "Take your son." She came in, fell at his feet and bowed to the ground. Then she took her son and went out. (2 Kings 4:29–36)

Elisha delegated authority to Gehazi. He ordered, *"Tuck your cloak into your belt, take my staff in your hand and run"* (v. 29). As Gehazi raced to the home of the Shunammite woman, he probably thought it would be easy to raise the dead boy. "This may be the day that my master sees the extent of my destiny. I'll show him that I am a great prophet, probably even greater than he is," he may have thought.

However, verse thirty-one states that *"there was no sound or response"* when Gehazi laid Elisha's staff on the dead child. A staff in Jewish history represented authority. Gehazi had received delegated authority from his master. However, this authority, in and of itself, was not enough to resurrect the boy.

In dejection, Gehazi returned to Elisha with the disturbing news, *"The boy has not awakened"* (v. 31). As Elisha traveled to the Shunammite's home, I have no doubt that his mind was on his longtime Friend, the Lord Almighty. When he reached the house, he closed the door on his servant and the boy's mother so that he could have an intimate moment with his Friend (v. 33). Elisha knew in his heart that somehow he had to express to the Lord that His covenantal responsibility should be to co-labor with him so that the boy might come alive.

Elisha expressed his concern and identified with the plight of the boy by lying directly upon him. The flesh of the child became warm after this first act. However, the boy was not resurrected. Verse thirty-five states that Elisha *"turned away and walked back and forth in the room and then got on the bed and stretched out upon him once more. The boy sneezed seven times and opened his eyes."* God revived the boy after Elisha's second act.

Something powerful must have been conveyed to God in the second act. I submit to you that Elisha conveyed to his Friend the covenantal responsibility of agreeing that the raising of the boy would be mutually beneficial. When Elisha lay on the boy the first time and the child's body became warm, his act symbolized the acknowledgment of the covenantal token when it was first sliced in half. The dismembered animal's body was still warm prior to ratification. Elisha, pacing to and fro in the room, represented the party who sealed the covenantal token by walking between the animals. In essence, Elisha was reminding God of the covenantal walk. Elisha was probably saying to the Father as he walked to and fro, "I need your help, my Lord. Co-labor with me, O God!"

When Elisha lay his body over the child's body the second time, the Bible states, *"The boy sneezed seven times and opened his eyes"* (v. 35). God had been reminded of walking through the sliced animal and the act of sealing the covenant—and He revived the boy! In Scripture, the number seven represents perfection. God allowed the boy to sneeze seven times to convey to Elisha, "My covenant with you, O friend, is one of perfection. I'll never break it."

THE ETHICS OF THE COVENANT

Being used by the Lord is based on a system of His merits, not ours. We don't qualify ourselves by our good works to operate in the gifts of the Holy Spirit. We could never earn the right or purchase it at any price. After Peter and John had raised up the lame beggar in the name of Jesus, the crowds, filled with wonder and amazement, began clinging to Peter and John. Peter had an interesting response. He said to them, *"Men of Israel, why does this surprise you? Why do you stare at us as if by our own power or godliness we had made this man walk?"* (Acts 3:12).

It's not your piety that qualifies you to move in the power of God. At the same time, when your relationship with God deteriorates, you lose the ability to co-labor with God. It's not so much a matter of clearing a minimum standard of personal righteousness. More likely, it is that when you stop walking with God, your interest and agenda changes. As the Scripture says, *"Can two walk together, except they be agreed?"* (Amos 3:3 KJV). In other words, if you choose to live an immoral, unholy, or spiritually insensitive life before God, you should not expect to sit in on a lot of board meetings with the Father. In that spiritual state, your interests are not God's interests.

Neither are manifestations of the spiritual gifts through a person's life to be viewed as spiritual merit badges signifying that the person is holy, perfected, or even mature in all areas of his or her life. I know of people with a lot of problems, even some serious character flaws, who are exercising the gifts of the Spirit. Many people wonder about this. An individual's personal problems don't necessarily discount the authenticity of the manifestation of the gift through him. But the operation of the gifts doesn't necessarily signify that he is always co-laboring with God. Even if your heart motive is wrong, God will sometimes still use you.

Moses' misuse of God's power and authority is a good example to consider. Moses had led the children of Israel out of their life of slavery in Egypt. At Kadesh the water ran out, and they all complained against Moses, wishing they were back in Egypt. God said to Moses,

> *Take the staff, and you and your brother Aaron gather the assembly together. Speak to that rock before their eyes and it will pour out its water. You will bring water out of the rock for the community so they and their livestock can drink. (Num. 20:8)*

However, there had been a lot of grumbling and complaining almost every step of the way, and by that time, Moses had had about all he could stand. So Moses obeyed the Lord, but only in part. He took the rod and said, *"Listen, you rebels, must we bring you water out of this rock?"* (v. 10). Moses then struck the rock twice with the rod, and water poured out.

Moses' anger affected his relationship with God. He lost touch with God's heart. A notable miracle took place through the hand of Moses, but that was not the end of the story. When he fell out of fellowship with God, he was no longer co-laboring with God. The consequence was that, though God still loved and used Moses, he was not permitted to enter the Promised Land.

When people do things, not out of a heart for God and His kingdom, but out of their own selfish desires, they may still appear to be blessed and used by God, but they may indeed have their reward in full. Those who find themselves morally or ethically compromised didn't get there without first becoming hardened and insensitive to the heart of God.

In chapter one, I wrote briefly about moving in the gifts of the Spirit with ease. A friendship relationship with Jesus through the continuing fellowship with the Holy Spirit is the lubrication that makes it all easy. Religion without relationship becomes incredibly boring, burdensome, and complicated. It is also devoid of passion and power, but God has called us to be joint-heirs, co-laborers, and friends.

When God chooses to co-labor with man, relational bonding through friendship and a covenant is the path that grace creates. Being a dreamer or a visionary doesn't qualify you to operate in the supernatural. Being actively involved in ministry is not equivalent to friendship with God. Nor does a relationship with a mighty man of God give you access to co-labor with the Father. The level of your relationship with Jesus Christ alone establishes the degree to which God co-labors with you in the operation of the grace gifts.

——Chapter 5——

The Purpose
of the Gifts

—————*Chapter 5*—————

The Purpose
of the Gifts

*Now to each one the manifestation
of the Spirit is given for the common good.
—1 Corinthians 12:7*

The kingdom of God is the outworking of God's plan and purpose, and everything in the kingdom moves toward those ends. Jesus said to the Pharisees who charged that He had cast out demons by the ruler of the demons, *"Every kingdom divided against itself is brought to desolation"* (Matt. 12:25 KJV). The point was very clear: neither Satan's kingdom nor God's kingdom is divided against itself, for it could not endure if it were so.

Everything that God does and everything that Satan does is oriented toward an objective, and that principle never wavers. God is not like humans, on-purpose sometimes and off-purpose other times. He's never weary, He's never bored, and He never takes a vacation.

Jesus went on to say, *"If I cast out devils by the Spirit of God, then the kingdom of God is come unto you"* (v. 28 KJV). In other words, when God manifests His power, it is always to establish His kingdom and accomplish His purpose. It is for this reason that the true nature of a ministry is judged by its fruit. The results are evaluated with regard to how they accomplish

God's purposes, because that is what true manifestations of the Spirit always do.

In the same way, the gifts of the Holy Spirit are always to focus on and function around God's eternal objectives. They are not given to entertain, to make church services more exciting, or to promote individuals and their ministries.

The Holy Spirit desires to use people who are more passionate about the purposes of God and His kingdom and less concerned about how it makes them look. Some people desire to move in the gifts of the Spirit primarily to be seen of men. Others seem to have a false sense of humility and think they could never be worthy enough or spiritual enough. Consequently, they would never dare to consider the fact that God might want to use them to manifest His power and presence.

Whether it is pride and selfish ambition or an inverted pride that masquerades as humility, both focus more on the perception of one's own self-worth than on the purposes of God. Both kinds of people need to get their eyes off themselves. The manifestation of a spiritual gift is not about you, the promotion of your ministry, or your own spiritual credentials; it is about the Holy Spirit's great desire to fulfill the purposes of the kingdom.

THE REDEMPTIVE FOCUS OF THE GIFTS

One facet of God's purpose is that He *"wants all men to be saved and to come to a knowledge of the truth"* (1 Tim. 2:4). Every gift God gives, including the nine gifts of the Holy Spirit listed in 1 Corinthians 12, has been soaked in the redemptive blood of His Son. Whenever the gifts are isolated from their redemptive character by the human vessel, they become a sideshow that lacks eternal substance. But when the gifts are allowed to operate from that reference point of God's redemptive purposes, the far-reaching hand of God is going to establish eternal changes in the lives of hurting people, and souls will always be added to the kingdom. The orchestration of the gifts of the Spirit will produce results that "work the work" of redemption.

Luke recorded in the book of Acts:

The Purpose of the Gifts

The apostles performed many miraculous signs and wonders among the people....More and more men and women believed in the Lord and were added to their number.　(Acts 5:12, 14)

Although the church has progressed two thousand years from this particular incident, the purpose of the gifts has not changed. I have personally witnessed the redemptive nature of the gifts. In fact, quite a few of the young converts in my church came to the Lord through the manifestation of the gifts of the Spirit.

A young woman in her early twenties came to one of our meetings. Judging from her facial expressions and her participation in the praise and worship portion of the service, she was apparently not enjoying our relationship with Christ. However, following the preaching of the Word, the Lord directed me to call her forward and minister to her through the gifts. As she walked toward the altar area, I knew within my spirit that something powerful was about to occur. As she stood in front of me with her back toward the congregation, immediately God spoke a word of knowledge to me regarding her past.

"You're a backslider!" I said to her. "Young lady, I am hearing a lot of singing in the spirit coming from your heart. In the days of your youth, you ministered to the Lord in song. However, for several years now you have turned your back on the Lord. He says He misses your singing, and He wants to hear your voice in His throne room once again."

Suddenly, the young woman broke down and started sobbing bitterly. God, through the gifts, had read her like a book. After she regained control of herself, I asked her if she would like to rededicate her life to Christ.

"Yes!" she quickly responded.

God, through the gifts, threw out His redemptive net and reconciled one of His wayward children to Himself.

Gifts without Boundaries

The gifts of the Holy Spirit always bear witness to the truth of the Gospel. When the manifestation bears witness, one of two things will happen: either a seed is sown or watered in the individual's heart, or conversion occurs. Paul commented on the effect of prophecy that works in such a fashion:

> *But if an unbeliever or someone who does not understand comes in while everybody is prophesying, he will be convinced by all that he is a sinner and will be judged by all, and the secrets of his heart will be laid bare. So he will fall down and worship God, exclaiming, "God is really among you!"*
>
> *(1 Cor. 14:24–25)*

The unbeliever is *"convinced by all"* and is *"judged by all."* These two verbs together imply the deep probing work and conviction of the Holy Spirit in people's lives. Dr. Gordon Fee, in *The New International Commentary on the New Testament,* says that lying behind this conviction is the Old Testament view that one is exposed before the living God through the prophetic word, even as Elijah confronted the evil King Ahab, or as Nathan confronted King David about the murder of Uriah.[1]

The truth of the Gospel is not relegated only to believers; God wants to talk to sinners as well. One problem is that most Christians believe that, in order for the gifts to function, we have to get away behind closed doors, excluding ourselves from the unbelievers. "You prophesy to me, and I'll prophesy to you," is normally the unspoken mindset of such a congregation.

However, the most powerful and effective demonstrations of spiritual gifts in the New Testament occurred in settings, both public and private, that were outside the gathering places of believers. The ministry of the apostles is summarized in the last verse of Mark's gospel: *"Then the disciples went out and preached everywhere, and the Lord worked with them and confirmed his word by the signs that accompanied it"* (Mark 16:20). Their preaching that was confirmed by the demonstration of the miraculous was not behind closed doors but was in the public places. This happened in spite of the fact that the Christians were usually outnumbered by the unbelievers.

Now, there is nothing wrong with enjoying Jesus with other Christians. However, you confine His abilities when you define His boundaries. Once the Holy Spirit used me in the word of knowledge to minister to an unbelieving teenager some things that occurred in her young life. The word described her family background as one of physical abuse and severe emotional turmoil. The word also stated that she was questioning God's existence and why, if He existed, these things had happened to her.

She began to cry, and she then asked me, "How did you know those things about me?" I told her quite frankly that it was God who spoke to my heart about her and, aside from that, I knew absolutely nothing about her. She did not accept the Lord at that time. But, God's name was vindicated, and a seed was planted in her heart, affirming His restorative love and protective ability.

A friend of mine shared a wonderful illustration of a gracious deliverance he received through the gift of prophecy. He was coming home late one night to his apartment in Brooklyn. Suddenly a robber jumped out of the dark right in front of him and announced, "Stick 'em up; give me all your money right now!" As the gun was pointed at him, the only thing that came to his mind was to trust God in the midst of this life-threatening encounter.

Instantly, my friend began to prophesy to the robber. The prophetic word centered on the robber's mother, who had prayed for his salvation and who constantly talked with him about his need for the Lord. The robber was frightened and said, "How did you know those things? I'm out of here! This is too crazy!" My friend was spared from being robbed and possibly harmed because he believed that spiritual gifts have no boundaries. They function equally well inside or outside of the church walls. I would love to end the story by saying that the robber was born again that night, but that was not the case. He simply ran back into the darkness.

Spiritual gifts are, of course, much more typical within the walls of the church. But the effect of manifestations of spiritual gifts outside the church can be incredible. God's desire is that we not hide our candle under a bushel basket; rather, He wants us to let our light shine before all men. We can never change the world when we are isolated from it.

RECAPTURING LIFE'S PURPOSE AND DIRECTION

The purpose of spiritual gifts is not only to bring people to the point of salvation, but also to bring them back to God's purpose for their lives or to move them along in God's plan.

Once I was ministering with the aid of an interpreter to a church in northern Germany. A young couple in the congregation were having terrible difficulties in their marriage. Divorce papers had already been filed with their attorney, and the process was to be finalized that very week. The stress and strain of it all had been so great that the man's wife had made arrangements to enter a mental institution for people overwhelmed with psychological and emotional problems. Both were still coming to the church periodically—coming separately, that is. I had known nothing about this situation until after the last evening service when they received personal ministry via the gifts of the Spirit.

They were both there that Saturday evening. But the young man, who played one of the percussion instruments for the music team, left after the praise and worship segment of the service had finished. One of my associates preached that evening, and I was leading the team in personal ministry afterward. I felt led by the Spirit to issue this invitation through the interpreter: "Those of you having tension and struggles in your marriage and who are on the verge of divorce or separation, come forward."

While fifty to seventy-five people began to move to the front, this young wife went out and called her husband, insisting that he return. After they both finally made their way to the front of the church, I began to minister to them through several of the gifts of the Spirit—prophecy, the word of knowledge, the word of wisdom, and the discerning of spirits.

I gave the young woman a word of knowledge about some of the issues in her childhood, particularly how she had been abused. This information helped her to understand why she and her husband had related to each other as they had. It also revealed to both of them the underlying cause of their difficulties. They both broke down and wept bitterly. In the brief course of ministry, their hearts were melted, and they were reconciled there on the spot. After that service, they had to go back to the attorneys and tear up all the divorce papers. The woman was able to have all the arrangements for her stay in the mental institution canceled.

As the evening meeting came to a close, I walked away wondering what would have happened over the years to that couple if the supernatural had not been unlocked. How many other marriages would have fallen apart? How many lives of siblings, children, grandchildren, and friends would have been psychologically traumatized by the wife if she had been institutionalized and not delivered? How much money would have been redirected from the kingdom of God to pay for medical doctors, clinical psychologists, and legal fees for attorney involvement with strained family matters? And, how many saints would have lived a defeated spiritual life if no one had helped them to obtain victory? Spiritual gifts are tools provided to the church by the Lord to deliver and keep His bride, the saints.

That is the redemptive purpose of the gifts. It's not just bringing people to salvation, but also restoring them to the purpose of God for their lives. The preaching of the Word was good, but it didn't do everything that night in Germany. The worship didn't do it either. It was the manifestation of the spiritual gifts that got this particular couple back on track.

Redemption involves restoration and reconciliation. The Holy Spirit uses the manifestation of His gifts to restore broken relationships and to bring people back to intimacy with the Father, and such is the purpose and function of all the gifts of the Spirit.

THE UNCOMFORTABLE GIFTS OF THE SPIRIT

One of greatest things about the revelatory gifts is that they simply let people know that God has not forgotten them, that He is intimately acquainted with their situation, and that they are not alone. That kind of information really causes one's faith to soar, and there is nothing that can be more comforting or encouraging. Paul, writing to the church in Corinth, commented on the purpose of the prophetic utterance: *"But everyone who prophesies speaks to men for their strengthening, encouragement and comfort"* (1 Cor. 14:3). All of the gifts exist to edify or build up the church as a whole, as well as each individual member.

Some people have read that verse and have wrongfully concluded that all the spiritual gifts, especially the revelatory gifts, are to make us feel good all the time. In other words, every prophecy, word of knowledge, or word of wisdom should be positive and uplifting. That's not necessarily the case. Knowing that God is intimately acquainted with all of our ways may be comforting to some, but not to others, especially to those who are headed away from Him.

The Greek word translated here as "comfort" is *parakaleo*. The same word is in other places translated as "beseech" and has a much stronger force than the word for "ask." W. E. Vine, in *An Expository Dictionary of New Testament Words,* comments on the use of *parakaleo,* saying that it means, "to entreat, to admonish, to urge one to pursue some course of conduct (always prospective, looking to the future, in contrast to the meaning *to comfort*)."[2]

Words from the Holy Spirit that exhort can be corrective and very straightforward. The Lord does not dance around critical issues as do some people. The gifts of 1 Corinthians 12 are outward manifestations of the same Spirit who convicts every sinner and has converted every believer. The same Spirit whose purpose it is to *"convict the world of guilt in regard to sin and righteousness and judgment"* (John 16:8), manifests His will through the exercising of the gifts. Light knows all about darkness and often bears witness against it through the gifts.

One of the hardest prophetic messages I have had to deliver came to me in an unusual way, a revelation with a revelation. God gave me a dream, and in the dream I had a vision of two men who were frequent visitors to my church. In the vision I saw that the men had entered into a homosexual relationship with one another. I also saw the man who was the less aggressive of the two in terms of sexuality, whisper to me in such a way that the other man could not hear. I was told by him that the more aggressive man was getting ready to go after some of the teenage boys in the church. "Be careful," he said to me. Then I woke up.

"What am I going to do with this?" I thought to myself. Dreams come in shadowy language and often speak of things that are to come. So I committed the matter to prayer for a number of days. In such cases, it's not enough to just get the information. I wanted to know the mind and heart of God on what to do with the information. I had to deal with the reality that these men had professed Christ years ago and were living a consistent Christian life from all outward appearances. They had significant positions of leadership in their churches, and the Christian community knew them to be model saints.

Finally, I approached the two men and shared my dream. Both of them began to weep. The prophetic dream awakened their consciences. They admitted that my dream was accurate. They had fallen into a sinful relationship with one another. Prior to the last month, only one of them had ever had a homosexual encounter, and this occurred several years prior to his accepting the Lord.

The prophetic revelation did not seem very comforting to them. It was an exhortation aimed at saving them and others. Prophecy can be very direct and confrontational, but it is always for a redemptive purpose, even if it does not seem so at the time. The yoke of bondage was very strong in this situation. It was the prophetic revelation that dramatically communicated the Father's urgency and His desire to embrace them as His children. In this case, I was able to lead them in a prayer of repentance and got them involved in counseling.

Bearing Witness to the Truth

I have noticed that, in very many cases, a supernatural word of knowledge, wisdom, or prophecy will merely confirm or reiterate the very thing that the Holy Spirit has been trying independently to impress on the heart of the believer. The character of the vocal gifts is that they are an external parallel to the work that the Holy Spirit is doing through the inner voice. The same Spirit is trying to get His message across to the individual.

So then, a word from God is often a confirmation of the inner voice that has been speaking. Other times it is simply a dramatic means by which the Holy Spirit speaks very loudly, often because the person has been turning a deaf ear to His inner voice. Usually that happens because people don't want to hear what He wants to say. They would like to hear God speak to them, but only as long as He doesn't bring up a particular subject.

After I had finished preaching one day in a church in Paterson, New Jersey, I pointed to a woman who was sitting close to the front and said, "You just said in your heart that this is your last service in this church—then you're out of here. The Lord says, 'You're not out of here, because I've planted you here.'"

I had not met or known the woman previously, but afterward she told me that, in the church's restroom that morning, she had said those very words to herself. She also admitted that God had been trying to get that message to her, but she had been previously unwilling to receive it.

Just imagine the relief one gains when God Himself edifies (builds up), exhorts (advises), and comforts (consoles) an individual in the midst of an intense trial. Recently, our church hosted a special series of meetings in which two speakers were invited to minister to our body. One of the young men in the congregation was undergoing a problem with depression. (One of the luxuries of being a pastor is that you get to know people's problems very quickly. Before God has a chance to tell you, they tell you!) The young man's depression resulted from guilt associated with his inability to comfort his family back home in Nigeria at the time of his uncle's death.

During the course of the meetings, one of the ministers prophesied to him, "God is lifting the depression and guilt that has been plaguing you as a result of the death of one of your relatives." The minister had no foreknowledge of this brother's situation! God had revealed these comforting words to the man of God through the gifts.

As I sat there, witnessing God in action, it was as if I were hearing the words of the prophet Isaiah in the prophetic word coming forth: *"The Sovereign LORD has given me an instructed tongue, to know the word that sustains the weary"* (Isa. 50:4).

Building the Church

Much has been written about church growth over the past decade. In fact, most Christian bookstores now have a special shelf among their pastoral aids designated for this new branch of study. C. Peter Wagner, one of the leading church growth experts, has even authored a book entitled, *Your Spiritual Gifts Can Help Your Church Grow.*[3]

There is sufficient documentation that the gifts of the Spirit, as well as one's natural gifts, can help the local church to grow. However, the words of Luke, quoted earlier, are worth repeating to validate this point:

> *The apostles performed many miraculous signs and wonders among the people....More and more men and women believed in the Lord and were added to their number.* *(Acts 5:12, 14)*

Through the manifestation of the gifts of the Spirit, the Jerusalem church experienced phenomenal growth. Such responses to the gifts were not uncommon in those days; nor should they be in ours. God's purpose for the gifts includes both growing the church numerically and maturing it as the bride of Christ. The prescription for such growth and maturity is in the epistle to the Ephesians:

> *Speaking the truth in love, we will in all things grow up into him who is the Head, that is, Christ. From him the whole body, joined and held together by every supporting ligament, grows and builds itself up in love.* *(Eph. 4:15–16)*

The Scriptures also say that *"to each one the manifestation of the Spirit is given for the common good"* (1 Cor. 12:7), and *"each one should use whatever gift he has received to serve others, faithfully administering God's grace in its various forms"* (1 Pet. 4:10). So the question is this: Are you a properly working part of the body of Christ? Are you a good steward of the manifestation of the Spirit that is given to you? If not, what's stopping you—sin, fear, procrastination, unbelief, insecurity, unworthy feelings, or just that you've been waiting for the Holy Spirit to move on His own through you without your participation? Whatever it is, why don't you lay those obstacles down before the Lord? Say to Him, "Here I am Lord, with all my problems and hesitations. Take me, and use Your gift through me to build Your kingdom."

——Chapter 6——

An Overview
of the Gifts

An Overview
of the Gifts

Now about spiritual gifts, brothers,
I do not want you to be ignorant.
—1 Corinthians 12:1

I t is hard for Christians today, with almost twenty centuries
of Christianity behind them, to understand the degree to
which first century Jews revered the prophets. God Himself
had spoken to and through Elijah, Elisha, Isaiah, Jeremiah,
Ezekiel, and others. He revealed Himself to Abraham and even
face-to-face to Moses, God's servant through whom some of the
greatest miracles in history were performed. The Spirit of God
was on these few individuals, and so, not only did they foretell
the future and deliver God's message, they also performed astounding miracles. They were not thought of as gods, as they
surely would have been in pagan cultures. Nevertheless, they
were, to say the very least, in the most exclusive of all categories. Everything in Judaism revolved around them; they were
the prophets!

The Prophets, a classical work on Old Testament prophets
by Abraham Heschel, says, "The prophet is not only a prophet.
He is also a poet, preacher, patriot, statesman, social critic,
moralist....The prophet is not a mouthpiece, but a person; not
an instrument, but a partner, an associate of God."[1] Given that

understanding, how it must have caused the Jews' ears to tingle when Peter stood up on the Day of Pentecost to explain the meaning of the outpouring of the Holy Spirit! He quoted the prophet Joel and said,

> *In the last days, God says, I will pour out my Spirit on all people. Your sons and daughters will prophesy, your young men will see visions, your old men will dream dreams. Even on my servants, both men and women, I will pour out my Spirit in those days, and they will prophesy.* (Acts 2:17–18)

The promise was that, when God poured out His Spirit, every person in His kingdom would experience on a small scale what the Old Testament prophets had experienced. What He had done in and through the prophets, He would do in and through those who were just regular members of the body of Christ. Incredible!

Jesus, when talking to two disciples of John the Baptist, put John in the same category with the prophets and even said that *"there is not a greater prophet than John the Baptist"* (Luke 7:28 KJV). But He also went on to say, in the same verse, *"Yet the one who is least in the kingdom of God is greater than he."*

So then, the gifts of the Holy Spirit are not to be seen as some new thing that God began to do on the Day of Pentecost. The Old Testament prophets exercised the gifts of the Spirit. The difference now is that same thing is happening, at least potentially, through every believer, not just through some. The members of the body of Christ are simply continuing on in the spiritual ministry of the prophets, proclaiming the message and demonstrating the power of God.

Since the turn of the century, many books have been written to aid the body of Christ in understanding the mechanics of the spiritual gifts. These works cite Scripture passages in which the gifts are discussed and also give modern illustrations to authenticate their continued existence. Some of these works contain great insights and thoroughly convey information regarding the operation of each gift.

However, most of these books concentrate on how the gifts operate rather than on how an individual can move in the gifts.

It is the intent of this book to expose the reader to the experiential dimension of the gifts. In order to do that, it is important to establish an overview of how each of the gifts referred to in 1 Corinthians 12 operates.

Please keep in mind that the goal of this chapter is to give you a general overview, not an account laced with heavy revelation. Before one can move in the gifts, a good understanding of their mechanics is required.

In his first letter to the Corinthians, the apostle Paul listed nine distinctive gifts of the Holy Spirit. Obviously, the expression of the gifts didn't begin with his writing of the letter. The gifts were already being exercised by the Spirit through the church. Paul simply recorded for the Corinthians what was happening in every place where the presence of the Holy Spirit was being manifested through the members of the church.

> *Now there are diversities of gifts, but the same Spirit. And there are differences of administrations, but the same Lord. And there are diversities of operations, but it is the same God which worketh all in all. But the manifestation of the Spirit is given to every man to profit withal. For to one is given by the Spirit the word of wisdom; to another the word of knowledge by the same Spirit; to another faith by the same Spirit; to another the gifts of healing by the same Spirit; to another the working of miracles; to another prophecy; to another discerning of spirits; to another divers kinds of tongues; to another the interpretation of tongues: but all these worketh that one and the selfsame Spirit, dividing to every man severally as he will.* (1 Cor. 12:4–11 KJV)

In this portion of Scripture, there are nine charismatic gifts listed. Each functions independently, and each is distinctly different from the others. The emphasis of the above passage is on the distinction of the gifts, for to one is given a certain gift and to one is given another gift.

Each gift will be manifested by the Holy Spirit in various ways, depending on the individual. Differing levels of supernatural expression can also be evidenced, based upon the maturity of the believer, the other gifts and ministries he or she possesses, and the situation. Since a single gift can be expressed in various ways, you could say that there are actually nine groups of supernatural manifestations, rather than nine gifts of the Spirit. We need not argue about semantics, however, as long as we realize that one gift can be exhibited in a variety of ways.

THE WORD OF WISDOM

The word of wisdom, along with the other eight charismatic gifts, is supernatural in nature. For this reason, Paul wrote, *"Now concerning spiritual* [supernatural] *gifts, brethren, I would not have you ignorant"* (1 Cor. 12:1 KJV). If Paul did not want the Corinthian church to be ignorant regarding the manifestations of the Holy Spirit, one can easily conclude that God desires us to have a working knowledge of these gifts today.

The Scriptures teach that there are three distinct types of wisdom apart from the word of wisdom:

- Natural wisdom: the ability of an unbeliever or believer to make good judgments in specific situations, based upon knowledge, learning, and so on. (See Luke 16:1–8; Proverbs 1:8–9; 12:8.)

- Satanic wisdom: the ability of Satan to exercise knowledge, learning, and insight into his affairs, as well as the affairs of those out of fellowship with God. (See Ezekiel 28:11–12, 17; James 3:14–17.)

- The wisdom of the recreated spirit: the ability of a child of God to draw from the wisdom of God through prayer and the study of His Word. (See 1 Corinthians 2:6–7; James 1:5; Proverbs 4:4–13.)

The word of wisdom, as a gift of the Holy Spirit, is a fraction or a fragment of God's wisdom, received supernaturally and delivered naturally. This gift, when in operation, provides insight regarding people, places, and things. Since the very meaning of the word *wisdom* connotes insight into the planning of future events, the gift provides a gracious deliverance through the revelation of facts about certain situations and the outcome of events. This is knowledge which our limited human intellect cannot perceive without God's aid.

Wisdom is often futuristic, but not in the sense that prophecy is futuristic. It is distinguished from prophecy in that prophecy informs you of what will happen in the future. The word of wisdom provides supernatural insight on how to deal with what will happen. When Paul first visited Corinth, he received great opposition, to the point that even his life had been threatened. He had, perhaps, concluded that it was time to move on, when he received a supernatural word of wisdom by means of a vision.

> *One night the Lord spoke to Paul in a vision: "Do not be afraid; keep on speaking, do not be silent. For I am with you, and no one is going to attack and harm you, because I have many people in this city." So Paul stayed for a year and a half, teaching them the word of God.* (Acts 18:9–11)

The wisdom of God was that, even though every indication was that it was too dangerous for Paul to stay, he would be safe in Corinth.

The word of wisdom may provide insight on how one may gracefully escape current dilemmas and precarious situations. When God told Samuel to anoint one of Jesse's sons as king because He had rejected Saul, Samuel feared for his life. He knew that if he walked into Bethlehem announcing the primary intention of his visit, King Saul would have his head.

As Samuel relayed his concern to the Lord, God gave him a word of wisdom: *"The LORD said, 'Take a heifer with you and say, "I have come to sacrifice to the LORD"'"* (1 Sam. 16:2). Again, as always, a mere fraction of God's wisdom secured deliverance for one of His servants.

Another example of the word of wisdom is in the New Testament. Jesus told His disciples, *"But when they arrest you, do not worry about what to say or how to say it. At that time you will be given what to say"* (Matt. 10:19).

Stephen, not one of the Twelve but certainly a disciple who had the same Spirit within him, was a man who moved mightily in the gifts of the Spirit. He was, according to the biblical account, *"full of God's grace and power"* and *"did great wonders and miraculous signs among the people"* (Acts 6:8). Stephen was called before the synagogue where the leaders began to argue against him, *"but they could not stand up against his wisdom or the Spirit by whom he spoke"* (v. 10). In this instance, the gift manifested itself in a more protracted, conversational, or ser-monic form as Stephen gave a defense of the Christian faith.

As the young prophet Samuel ministered unto the Lord, God gave him a word of wisdom regarding his master, Eli (1 Sam. 3:10–14). The fragment of God's wisdom, in this instance, manifested itself through a vision to Samuel. Note that God spoke of future events. *"And the LORD said to Samuel: 'See, I am about to do something in Israel that will make the ears of everyone who hears of it tingle'"* (v. 11). When God speaks His wisdom to man, the awesomeness of the revealed information will cause man's ears to tingle!

THE WORD OF KNOWLEDGE

He told her, "Go, call your husband and come back." "I have no husband," she replied. Jesus said to her, "You are right when you say you have no husband. The fact is, you have had five husbands, and the man you now have is not your hus-band."
(John 4:16–18)

This famous account of the meeting between Jesus and the Samaritan woman at the well contains a reservoir of truth re-garding His ability to transform a sinner. It is also an example of spiritual gifts in operation. The word of knowledge was mani-fested when Christ made this personal comment to the woman: *"The fact is, you have had five husbands, and the man you now have is not your husband"* (v. 18). The supernatural exposure of the woman's marital past and her present sinful state resulted in her salvation and subsequent ministry. She began sharing the Good News with the other Samaritans.

The word of knowledge is the supernatural exposure of the mind of God regarding something in the past or present. The fragment of information may relate to a person, place, thing, feeling, or idea. The operation of this gift, however, is neither an acute sensitivity to human behavior nor spiritual revelations based on already known facts about a person. It is verbally sharing a fragment of God's knowledge. There are also three different types of knowledge apart from the word of knowledge:

- Natural knowledge: the ability of an unbeliever or believer to understand facts, information, or discoveries gained through experience or study. (See Daniel 9:2; Proverbs 1:1, 4; 2 Timothy 2:15.)

- Satanic knowledge: the skill, talent, or power of Satan to gather data and information or to make discoveries about his kingdom, as well as the affairs of those in and outside of his reign. (See Genesis 3:1–5; Job 1:6–12.)

- The knowledge of the recreated spirit: the ability of a believer to seek out from God, through worship, prayer, and fasting, specific knowledge about kingdom business. (See Daniel 9:3–4, 21–22; Acts 27:21–26; 2 Peter 3:18.)

An example of the word of knowledge in the Old Testament occurs at a point in history when the king of Syria was warring against Israel. The invading king was convinced that he had a spy in his midst because every plan he made was conveyed to the king of Israel. Finally, he was told by one of his servants, *"Elisha, the prophet who is in Israel, tells the king of Israel the very words you speak in your bedroom"* (2 Kings 6:12).

THE GIFT OF FAITH

The Bible speaks of several different types of faith: saving faith, faith confessions, ordinary faith, the prayer of faith, and the gift of faith.

Saving faith is what enabled every believer, while still in a sinful state, to call upon Jesus for salvation (Rom. 3:21–23). Faith confessions are the declarations of God's revealed promises as found in Scripture. According to Mark 11:23, we have the right to stand in faith against obstacles that hinder us from experiencing the blessings of the Lord. The gift of faith differs in definition and function from the other categories of faith. This gift is passive, yet powerful.

You can logically divide the nine gifts into three groups: revelatory gifts, inspirational gifts, and power gifts. The gift of faith would be in the category of the power gifts, along with the gifts of healing and the working of miracles. An easy way to distinguish between the gift of faith and the working of miracles is that the working of miracles performs a miracle while the gift of faith speaks it.

Often, when the gift of faith is in operation, we don't acknowledge its presence, simply because something is quietly spoken in faith by the person operating in the gift. The outcome, a miracle, is so powerful that we inadvertently ignore the proclamation of faith that accompanied it.

On their first missionary journey, Paul and Barnabas had sailed from Antioch to the island of Cyprus. Sergius Paulus, the Roman proconsul, had summoned Paul and Barnabas. He had also arranged for Elymas, a magician and a sorcerer who was also known as Bar-Jesus, to be present. The proconsul was interested in hearing the Gospel, but Elymas opposed Paul and Barnabas in order to turn the proconsul away from their message. Paul turned his attention to Elymas, said a few words about the deceit in his heart, and declared, *"Now the hand of the Lord is against you. You are going to be blind, and for a time you will be unable to see the light of the sun"* (Acts 13:11). Paul's words, inspired by the gift of faith, resulted in the miracle of temporary blindness coming upon Bar-Jesus the sorcerer. Needless to say, the proconsul became a believer.

The gift of faith is not only for curses, but also for blessings. Often, this gift works in conjunction with other gifts of the Spirit (i.e., the word of wisdom, the word of knowledge, and the discerning of spirits).

The Lord once spoke a word of knowledge to me in the midst of a meeting regarding a woman who was unable to bear children. She and her husband had been trying for several years to have a child, without success. Suddenly I felt within my spirit an assurance that was absolute. I knew God wanted to give her a child. The gift of faith causes a heavenly assurance to well up within the spirit of the agent who is being used by God.

The power of God came upon me, and I declared to her, "By this time next year you will embrace a child!" Several months later, she attended one of our meetings wearing a maternity dress! Praise the Lord! God allowed me to speak a miracle upon His daughter through the gift of faith.

Notice that when the gift of faith was activated in Paul, the Bible uses the term *"filled with the Holy Spirit"* (Acts 13:9) to describe Paul's response to God's revealed desires concerning the sorcerer. God wanted to deal strongly with the false prophet, and He indicated His vehemence to Paul.

There are two acronyms that describe the operation of the gift of faith: FAITH is Full Assurance In The Heart, and it is also Free Access Into The Heavens. The gift of faith is characterized by the supernatural ability experienced within a brief moment of time, enabling a person to have extraordinary faith in God.

GIFTS OF HEALING

The gifts of healing are the supernatural manifestation of God's healing and restorative abilities. There is a lot of things being said these days about alternative means of healing, many of them claiming that they can show you how to tap into a source of spiritual power. For example, eastern religions and their practices of incantation are leading many astray in their attempt to access supernatural healing. There are also hundreds of books and seminars about healing through the use of natural foods and vitamins.

In the '80s and '90s, people started becoming more and more health-conscious because of a growing distrust in conventional medical practice, not to mention the escalating expense. Certainly, God wants you to take care of your body properly, for it is the temple of the Holy Spirit (2 Cor. 6:16). Unfortunately, in an attempt to gain health and healing, many have run to the wrong sources for help (e.g., witchcraft, the occult, and New Age spiritualism). If you are not cautious, a simple trip to your neighborhood health food store for a natural remedy could result in a new spiritual outlook on life.

Amid the array of questionable medical practitioners, eastern religions, New Age formulas, and the latest miracle herb,

God's healing power is still being experienced by many of His children. To the Canaanite woman who came to Jesus on behalf of her daughter, Jesus said that healing is the bread that belongs to the children of the kingdom (Matt. 15:22–28).

In response to a word of knowledge, a woman whose body was totally emaciated from cancer walked down the center aisle of a church. Moments before, a man of God had jumped out of his seat and run to the pastor to share with him how God had given him a word of knowledge that a woman would be healed of cancer.

The woman walked toward the altar area, not knowing what to expect. Her physicians had told her she had only a few months to live. The pastor and the brother who had received the word of knowledge prayed for her, and God miraculously healed her! When she returned to her doctors, they could find no trace of cancer in her body! Once again, God demonstrated Himself through the gifts of healing.

Supernatural healing can also take place through the ordinary faith of a believer (Mark 16:18), without the use of the gifts of healing. The method of ministry through which the gifts of healing can flow varies. Elisha told Naaman, the Syrian general, to go and dip himself in the Jordan River seven times. After a brief battle with his own pride, Naaman did so and was indeed healed (2 Kings 5).

Jesus spit in the dirt, made mud, and applied it to a blind man's eyes (John 9:6), and he received his sight. When Paul was shipwrecked on an island, he laid his hand on the father of the leading man of the island. The old man's fever and dysentery were immediately healed (Acts 28:8). The apostle James wrote to the church,

> *Is any one of you sick? He should call the elders of the church to pray over him and anoint him with oil in the name of the Lord. And the prayer offered in faith will make the sick person well; the Lord will raise him up. If he has sinned, he will be forgiven.* (James 5:14–15)

Following prayer and/or the laying on of hands, healing may be gradual or dramatic. God chooses the time factor in every case in accordance with His own will. Determining how a person is healed, whether through ordinary Christian faith or the charismatic gift, is not the most important issue. The point is that God heals people for His own glory!

THE WORKING OF MIRACLES

The New Dictionary of Theology states, "The word *miracle* comes from the Latin *miraculum,* meaning 'a wonder.' It suggests supernatural interference with nature or the course of events."[2] Consequently, the gift of the working of miracles occurs when God uses an individual to bring about a supernatural intervention in the natural order of things, so that His will may be accomplished.

The parting of the Red Sea was a supernatural intervention by God, who empowered Moses to deliver the children of Israel from the clutches of Pharaoh. The opening of the Red Sea was not a natural phenomenon. It was a specific act performed for a specific reason through a human agent.

Paul preached a long-winded sermon in Troas during which a young man named Eutychus fell into a deep sleep and fell out of a third-floor window and died.

> *Paul went down, threw himself on the young man and put his arms around him. "Don't be alarmed," he said. "He's alive!"...* [Then] *the people took the young man home alive and were greatly comforted.* (Acts 20:10, 12)

Through the gift of working of miracles, along with the gift of faith and, perhaps, gifts of healing, Paul worked a miracle. God can even use us to raise the dead if we have killed them with boring sermons!

When Elisha cut a stick and cast it into the water in an attempt to retrieve a sunken ax head from the Jordan River, the Bible states, *"And the iron did swim"* (2 Kings 6:6 KJV). How could a sunken ax head float to the top of the water simply as a result of a stick being thrown into the river? Obviously, it was a miracle. The laws of buoyancy were bypassed in this instance through the working of miracles.

THE GIFT OF PROPHECY

The word *prophesy* means "to speak or sing under divine inspiration." The message itself, the prophecy, may foretell or forth-tell God's intentions regarding a certain matter. When one prophesies, a clear, distinct idea from God is voiced to a congregation or an individual. The articulated message may contain information about the future or strong declarative thoughts centering around edification, exhortation, or comfort (1 Cor. 14:3).

Forth-telling is when one speaks decrees by the prompting of the Holy Spirit. This format of prophecy gives announcements, decisions, orders, or presentations for the present—a message that does not necessarily relate to things in the future. Foretelling, on the other hand, is a prophecy that deals with prognostications—predictions for the future that will bring change to present predicaments. This second mode also includes indications or signs intended to authenticate its truthfulness.

Several years ago I was speaking at a church-sponsored conference in Nigeria. At one of the evening meetings, I prophesied, "God is going to meet the financial needs of this church so that you can complete your building project, and before the meeting ends tonight, God will grant you a sign authenticating His promise. The sign will be that hundreds of people will receive the baptism of the Holy Spirit with the evidence of speaking in other tongues."

Now, you must realize that this part of Nigeria and the congregants of this particular church were extremely poor. Their church edifice had no roof, floor, windows, doors, restrooms, or electricity. Nevertheless, my prophetic word was foretelling what God wanted to do for these precious people.

Immediately following the sermon that night, I called up all those who had not as of yet experienced the baptism of the Holy Spirit. About two hundred and fifty to three hundred people responded and came toward the front of the sanctuary. After giving some brief instructions, I waved my hand across the audience, and hundreds of believers were filled with the Holy Spirit instantly. God's sign came to pass! Later on in that meeting and throughout the remainder of the conference, we were able to raise enough money to complete that phase of the building project. Praise God!

Prophecy is an inspirational gift, as is implied by its definition. A theological meaning of the word *inspiration* is "divine guidance or influence exerted directly upon the mind and soul of man." Thus, when an individual has a prophetic word to impart, the inference is that the Holy Spirit has divinely exerted influence upon that person.

The word *naba* is one of the Hebrew words used in the Old Testament to mean "to prophesy." Dr. David Blomgren, in his book, *Prophetic Gatherings in the Church*, cites this word as meaning "to bubble up, to gush forth, to pour forth." He adds, "Thus, the prophetic message pours forth from the anointed prophet [or spokesperson] as water from a fountain."[3] Therefore, the influence exerted on the child of God is an internal heightening of pressure born out of God's desire to share His thoughts with His people.

When this type of manifestation is occurring, the prophetic word feels like it is actually fermenting or effervescing in one's spirit. It is similar to soda in a can after it has been shaken aggressively. Incidentally, the timing in which a prophetic word is given has a lot to do with its effectiveness. If the timing of delivery is wrong (too late or too early), the word will not have the effect on the listener that it was intended to have. This is where mentoring from more seasoned believers can be beneficial.

Agabus was a prophet in the Jerusalem church. There are two references in the book of Acts to his prophetic ministry. The first is in Acts 11.

> *During this time some prophets came down from Jerusalem to Antioch. One of them, named Agabus, stood up and through the Spirit predicted that a severe famine would spread over the entire Roman world. (This happened during the reign of Claudius.)* (Acts 11:27–28)

Sometimes the Holy Spirit will inspire physical demonstrations to graphically illustrate a prophetic word. This same prophet is mentioned again in Acts 21.

After we had been there a number of days, a prophet named Agabus came down from Judea. Coming over to us, he took Paul's belt, tied his own hands and feet with it and said, "The Holy Spirit says, 'In this way the Jews of Jerusalem will bind the owner of this belt and will hand him over to the Gentiles.'"
(Acts 21:10–11)

This mode of prophesying is similar to the way Old Testament prophets occasionally delivered the word of the Lord. It was conveyed in physical deeds, as well as in word. Ahijah the Shilonite tore his new cloak to show how Solomon's kingdom would be disrupted (1 Kings 11:30), Isaiah walked naked and barefoot to show how the Egyptians would be led away by Assyria (Isa. 20:3–4), and Ezekiel mimicked the Babylonian siege of Jerusalem by laying siege himself to a replica of the city (Ezek. 4).[4] The degree of sensitivity one has toward God will affect how yielded one is to the Lord and the accompanying gestures he or she will be courageous enough to perform.

Having the gift of prophecy operative in one's life does not make one a prophet. The ministry of a prophet is an office in the church just as is the ministry of a pastor or teacher. It is one of the ascension ministry gifts listed in Ephesians 4:11. A prophet is usually a person in whom the Holy Spirit has for some time been perfecting and maturing the revelatory gifts. Though everyone can teach the Word, not everyone is recognized as being in the office of a teacher. Still, the gift of prophecy is one of the charismatic gifts (1 Cor. 12) that is accessible to every believer by means of the grace of God, not just to those who are recognized by the church as prophets.

Prophecy (personal or otherwise), whether delivered by a person in the office of a prophet or by any other member of the church, is a powerful tool when used properly. This is exactly why Paul stated, *"Follow the way of love and eagerly desire spiritual gifts, especially the gift of prophecy"* (1 Cor. 14:1).

THE GIFT OF DISCERNING OF SPIRITS

Discerning of spirits falls into the grouping of revelation gifts alongside the word of knowledge and the word of wisdom.

The word *discern* means "a clear discrimination; judging; judicial estimation." Thus, the term *discerning of spirits* denotes discrimination of spirits. Notice the word *spirit* appears in the plural form, *"spirits,"* in 1 Corinthians 12:10.

There are three categories of spirits: demonic spirits, human spirits, and spirits of God (e.g., seraphim, cherubim, angels, and so on). The implication here is that when one operates in the gift of discerning of spirits, insight regarding spiritual matters is not limited to just one category of spirits, but, rather, it includes the full spectrum of spirits.

One may ask, "What is the purpose of discerning of spirits?" In order for church leaders to protect the flock adequately, they must know who labors among them. When one can accurately discern the spiritual motivation of a person or group and the category (or categories) of spirits involved, then the necessary steps can be taken to deal properly with the situation, whether it is to honor those who serve with a pure heart or to guard against those with self-serving motives.

After Philip invited Nathanael to come and meet Jesus, the Bible records that *"when Jesus saw Nathanael approaching, he said of him, 'Here is a true Israelite, in whom there is nothing false'"* (John 1:47). The significance of Jesus' statement is that it was as a result of the manifestation of the gift of discerning of spirits. It is important that you realize Jesus' statement was not the gift; it was spoken as a result of what He discerned about Nathanael supernaturally. Discerning of spirits is the unveiling of information, promptings, or motivation by God about a spirit or spirits.

Nathanael made a radical confession of faith in Christ due to Jesus' ability to hone in on what was absolutely essential to the core of his being. He said to Jesus, *"Rabbi, you are the Son of God; you are the King of Israel"* (v. 49). Apparently, Nathanael prided himself (in a good way) on his personal ethics, morals, and integrity. So, when Jesus called him *"a true Israelite, in whom there is nothing false,"* he knew that Jesus had gained insight into his life supernaturally. The church would fare well if our leaders would know their parishioners early on through discerning of spirits. The value of the gift is not just for leaders, but all of us can benefit immensely through God opening our understanding to what is really going on in our personal worlds.

Paul, in response to a vision of a man saying, *"Come over to Macedonia and help us"* (Acts 16:9), arrived in Philippi with Silas and Luke. As they went from place to place preaching the Gospel, there was slave girl who followed them everywhere they went.

> *Once when we were going to the place of prayer, we were met by a slave girl who had a spirit by which she predicted the future. She earned a great deal of money for her owners by fortune-telling. This girl followed Paul and the rest of us, shouting, "These men are servants of the Most High God, who are telling you the way to be saved." She kept this up for many days. Finally Paul became so troubled that he turned around and said to the spirit, "In the name of Jesus Christ I command you to come out of her!" At that moment the spirit left her.* (vv. 16–18)

The slave girl who was following Paul was saying all the right words, but Paul discerned that she had a spirit of divination. Imagine the countless problems the young church in Philippi avoided by the gift of discerning of spirits operating through Paul.

Discerning of spirits presents facts regarding the activity of spirits. One can obtain these facts through hearing, smelling, or seeing (through visions and dreams) the spirit's presence. Elisha, the prophet who had the word of knowledge concerning the Syrian king's battle plans, was surrounded by the king's forces. The prophet, in response to his servant's fears, asked the Lord to open his servant's eyes. *"Then the LORD opened the servant's eyes, and he looked and saw the hills full of horses and chariots of fire all around Elisha"* (2 Kings 6:17). Apparently, Elisha was able to discern the spirits when they were unseen by all others.

Discerning of spirits is a supernatural gift, not natural discernment, faultfinding, street smarts, or sociological awareness. Natural discernment is possessed by everyone, albeit in varying levels of keenness and maturity. Natural discernment simply means that a person is able to detect or perceive with the eyes of the intellect; he is aware of distinctions and can discriminate among various things. Nowhere in this definition is there a hint of supernatural insight or activity. If you walk into a room after a couple has been arguing intensely with one another, more than likely you will feel a coldness about the room chemistry. They may try to cover up what has been taking place with a facade of friendliness and smiles, but you can still discern the spiritual atmosphere.

Faultfinding, I always say, is a gift of the flesh, and it can always be in full operation. Because it is a work of the flesh, faultfinding has no redemptive value and never can. Discerning of spirits, on the other hand, like all the other eight charismatic gifts, has redemptive purposes and actions.

There is a man in my church who has a Ph.D. in street smarts. Of course, there is no such degree, but if there was one, he would deserve it. When it comes to spotting phonies, potentially troublesome people, or sophisticated scams designed by drug addicts intended to land them some benevolence monies, he can always discern them. His track record is extremely accurate. However, this ability to be discriminate is not the result of the gift of discerning of spirits; rather, it comes through his experience on the street.

There has been much literature written on understanding body language. This science is simply a compilation of information gathered from sociological studies on human behavior. Much of it will provide us with factual information about people's behaviors, interpretations of common mannerisms, and so on. Yet, this is not a shade of or a reflection of discerning of spirits. If it were the same as the gift of discerning of spirits, one could simply study body language in order to operate in this charismatic gift.

The problem created by this non-biblical approach is that it contradicts the clear teaching of 1 Corinthians 12:11, which says, *"These are the work of one and the same Spirit, and he gives* [the charismatic gifts] *to each one, just as he determines."* There you have it, as I mentioned in chapter three: the gifts are distributed by God sovereignly and cannot be asked for through prayer, fasting, or any other means.

Several years ago, God allowed me to see a selfish, self-promoting spirit that was influencing a minister friend of mine.

In the natural, this minister was a determined, goal-oriented person. However, when God enabled me to see, through discerning of spirits, what was spiritually motivating this man, I realized that he would step on anyone to get where he wanted to go. Fame was his aim, and people were disposable if they rubbed him the wrong way. By assessing this minister's intentions properly, I was able to avoid any unhealthy encounters with him.

Discerning of spirits is a powerful and necessary tool for establishing the fear of God. An important point to be remembered is that once a demon, angel, or human spirit is exposed, judgment must follow. Judgment is not always bad. In fact, judgment simply means "the ability to make a decision or form an opinion objectively, authoritatively, and wisely." God allowed me to clearly discern my minister friend's motives so that I could be cautious in my dealings with him and know how to pray for him.

TONGUES AND INTERPRETATION

In a church I was visiting, the orchestra and worship leaders gradually brought a song to its close in response to the corporate prompting of the Lord. A quietness came over the entire assembly. Something was about to happen. Suddenly, a man in the rear of the sanctuary began to speak in an unknown language. As he spoke, it was as though everyone knew he was articulating a clear thought in some language foreign to the congregation. When he completed his message, a momentary pause occurred throughout the church. Everyone waited silently to see what would follow.

Immediately, a woman in the front began speaking some strong, declarative statements in English, the language of the congregation, as though she were interpreting the message previously given by the man. Her words indicated that she was speaking on God's behalf at that very moment.

After she concluded, the pastor of the church encouraged the assembly that they should not be alarmed. This occurrence is what the Bible refers to in 1 Corinthians 12:10 as *"different kinds of tongues"* and *"the interpretation of tongues."*

Different kinds of tongues and the interpretation of tongues are two inspirational gifts of the Spirit. They usually function together and, during such times, the outcome of the dual manifestation is similar to the gift of prophecy. The interpreted message edifies, exhorts, and comforts the church, while it also glorifies God.

When tongues occur in a public setting without interpretation, the situation is like that cited in the account of the Holy Spirit falling on the Day of Pentecost (Acts 2:4–11). When the one hundred and twenty people in the Upper Room were filled with the Holy Spirit, they began to speak in other tongues *"as the Spirit enabled them"* (v. 4). The onlookers included many foreigners dwelling in Jerusalem, such as Parthians, Cretes, and Arabians, who, when they heard these Galileans speaking in tongues, said, *"We hear them declaring the wonders of God in our own tongues!"* (v. 11).

One can readily understand that *tongues* means "languages." The gift of interpretation of tongues was not necessary in this case, because each of the onlookers heard his own native language distinctly and understood the message. God used the gift of different kinds of tongues as a sign of His redemptive abilities.

In a church setting, the Holy Spirit may influence the heart of man to speak in tongues to an individual or congregation. The person may speak forth God's message or heaven-inspired praises. The same individual or someone else then supernaturally interprets the previously spoken words through the gift of interpretation of tongues. Note that the message that follows the expression in tongues is referred to by the Bible as an interpretation, not a translation. An interpretation is an explanation of what was said, not necessarily a word-for-word rendering from tongues into the known language of the congregation.

Historically and in many modern-day churches, confusion occurs in corporate gatherings when the gift of different kinds of tongues is misused and misunderstood. The Scriptures teach that, once a believer receives the baptism of the Holy Spirit, the initial act that follows is the person's ability to speak in other tongues (Acts 10:44–46; 19:1–6). Paul referred to an individual's use of tongues in private as a prayer language, and the public use of tongues as a spiritual gift to work in conjunction with the interpretation of tongues (1 Cor. 14). However, in a public setting, if a message spoken audibly in tongues is actually a personal prayer (v. 2) or a declaration of praise (Acts 10:46), an interpretation is not to be expected. When used properly, these gifts are quite effective in building up a local church.

——Chapter 7——

The Internal
Operation of Grace

The Internal
Operation of Grace

Before they call I will answer;
while they are still speaking I will hear.
—Isaiah 65:24

N ow that the theological premise regarding the operation of the gifts of the Spirit has been established, let us explore how one can activate the gifts.

Have you ever stopped to think about the incredible technology of television? You can point a camera at an object or event, and through the wonder of satellites and microwave communications, the picture appears almost instantaneously in a living room on the other side of the world.

While most kids I grew up with were only interested in the content of the television programming, I had a burning desire to know how the television actually worked. My younger brother and I, two budding engineers, were never as concerned with what something did as we were with taking it apart to find out what made it tick. After all these years, I still look at things and wonder how they work. I have approached the gifts of the Spirit with that same kind of scientific curiosity.

When the gifts are being manifested, most people tingle with excitement and are overwhelmed at the wonder of the Holy Spirit expressing Himself in a visible, tangible way. They are so taken with what they can see externally that they seldom think about the internal mechanics of the vessel God uses. The question they should eventually get around to asking is, How and why does God work through that person?

Christians who think of spiritual gifts as sovereign acts of the Holy Spirit don't consider the internal dynamics because, for them, there are no internal dynamics. They assume that the gifts operate without any cooperation from human agents. On the other hand, there are those who still have an Old Testament mindset, assuming that the Holy Spirit only uses a very select few for such demonstrations of His power. They fail to understand that, as Joel prophesied, God would pour out His Spirit on all mankind, to both men and women, and that they would all move in the gifts of the Spirit (Joel 2:28–32; Acts 2:17–18). Unfortunately, these people walk away from meetings in which the Spirit is manifested, thinking, "God really used that person tonight, but I don't think I could ever be used like that."

Still, there are also those who, after witnessing the operation of the Spirit, understand that God is co-laboring with people. Consequently, they are motivated to learn how to move in the gifts. Proper teaching will enable them to see beyond the splendor of the manifestations so that they may begin to understand the mechanics that cause the supernatural occurrences.

INTERNAL MECHANICS OF SPIRITUAL GIFTS

In order to learn how to minister in the gifts from the perspective of grace, the mechanics of the operation must be understood. Consequently, the focus of this chapter is on the steps that occur and reoccur in every expression of biblical and modern-day manifestations of the spiritual gifts. Sometimes these steps are obvious, and at other times they are below the surface. In either case, they are not to be understood legalistically.

As I have said before, a relationship with God is the key to moving in deeper levels of the gifts. Each of these steps represents issues of your relationship with God, and each step is expressed in a question that the grace vessel must ask God.

SIX STEPS TO MOVING IN THE GIFTS

Let us now explore the six-step process of moving in the gifts through the vehicle of grace. When a believer endeavors to see God display His power, his motives must be pure. God's graciousness and God's will must be on his mind, not thoughts straying away from the Father's character. Remember, the gifts flow when God chooses to co-labor with man through the channel of a covenant. Man steps out of the covenantal, co-laboring relationship whenever he tries to manipulate God by quoting Scripture or using any other tactic. Sometimes people presumptuously step out into situations without inquiring of the Lord at all. They do so in order to create a crisis in which they think God will be "forced to move."

That is precisely what the prophets of Baal were doing on Mount Carmel. By cutting and torturing themselves to such a degree, they were, in effect, saying to their idol, "You must do something, or we're going to kill ourselves." God moves when we cooperate and co-labor with Him, and He will not be manipulated by anyone or by any means. Creating a crisis by our own presumption will not force God's hand. It will only get us into trouble.

In the spirit world, responses to questions, thoughts, or concerns can occur in a fraction of a second. God declares, *"Before they call I will answer; while they are still speaking I will hear"* (Isa. 65:24). In fact, a lengthy dialogue with God can take a moment's time! For example, the prophet Samuel had an extensive discussion with God in a fraction of time during the process of selecting one of Jesse's sons to be king (1 Sam. 16:4–13).

It is as though heaven is set up to handle the emergencies of men residing on earth. God does not need several hours or a day to think things over and respond accordingly. He knows what He wants to do at all times. Since the gifts of the Spirit operate through a co-laboring effort, and since God is omniscient, man is the only agent in the partnership who needs to ask questions about the most appropriate action. The questions to be posed to God are as follows.

121

God, What Is Your Will Regarding This Situation?

That's the first question in the process and one that must be answered before anything else can be done. If God does not want to respond to a situation in a way we feel is correct, I guarantee you that His will, not ours, will prevail. If Paul, on his own, had chosen to call down blindness upon Elymas the sorcerer, would he have become blind? Obviously not.

James and John observed that one particular village of the Samaritans refused to receive Jesus because He was traveling on His way to Jerusalem—on His way, that is, to be crucified. Having been instructed by Jesus on the authority they would possess in the kingdom of God, the two disciples were ready to call fire down from heaven upon this village. However, before trying to use their authority, the first thing they did was ask,

> *Lord, wilt thou that we command fire to come down from heaven, and consume them, even as Elias did? But he turned, and rebuked them, and said, Ye know not what manner of spirit ye are of. For the Son of man is not come to destroy men's lives, but to save them.* (Luke 9:54–56 KJV)

According to *The Interpreter's Bible*, the implication of Jesus' response was, "You do not know what is going on in my mind and heart and how utterly out of tune with my mood such words as those are."[1] These two disciples came to understand that power, authority, and the gifts of God flow, not just from an up-to-date relationship, but from an up-to-the-moment relationship. The gifts cannot operate in opposition to the will of God. Therefore, the Lord's will must be known!

We also have to be careful about preconceived notions of what God will or will not do. Peter was in Joppa when God showed him a vision of all kinds of unclean animals (Acts 10:9–16). In the vision, Peter was told to kill and eat. God was trying to tell the reluctant disciple to go to the house of Cornelius, a Gentile, and preach the Gospel. After two visions, an angelic visitation to Cornelius, and an outpouring similar to the Day of Pentecost, Peter was still reluctant to water baptize the Gentiles because of his hard-and-fast, preconceived notions. It's difficult to hear God's direction, no matter how spectacularly He speaks, when we are locked into our preconceptions of what God wants to do. We must lay aside our will, ideas, and agendas to most effectively ascertain His.

God, What Is on Your Heart?

Most people don't realize that the Father has moods. *The American College Dictionary* defines the word *mood* as "a frame of mind, or state of feeling, as at a particular time."[2] Having mood variations does not imply that one is fickle or that there is moral decay in one's character. God is not what we would call moody.

Almost all of the ancient, pagan world viewed the god or gods they believed in as petty, capricious, and easily given over to fits of rage and jealousy. If one did something that rubbed a god the wrong way or if the god simply woke up with a headache, the so-called deity might cause a volcano to erupt and wipe out the city. Consequently, pagan worshippers were always offering sacrifices to appease their god's anger because, in their minds, a god with an attitude would cause all kinds of terrible things to happen.

One of the problems with all these ancient, pagan religions was that their gods were little more than deified forms of humanity. In other words, the gods were created in man's image, with all the problems of mankind's nature. But God (with a capital *G*), who has revealed Himself through the Scriptures and through the person of Jesus Christ, is in His nature eternal, omnipresent, and unchangeable while being perfectly holy, righteous, and loving in His character. Human emotions are a reflection of God's nature and character because we are made in His image. Self-centered moodiness comes from mankind's fallen nature, while God's moods are emotions that are perfect expressions of His holiness and love.

To better understand the moods of God, examine the issue of worship. Sometimes God wants us to praise Him with a shout, while at other times He desires to hear a soft, majestic song. Sometimes He wants us to dance and other times to prostrate ourselves before Him. The reason for this is simply that God varies His moods.

The issue of God's mood is, therefore, important with regard to the expression of the gifts of the Spirit. Let's assume that you are in the midst of a dynamic service where the disposition of the Holy Spirit is clearly centered on "unity in the body." Would God suddenly direct someone to flow in the gift of prophecy and articulate a message on His provision for physical healing? Hardly. A prophetic message solely on physical healing would change the whole tone and mood of the meeting, and confusion would follow. God is not the author of confusion! In some meetings, God chooses to emphasize the gifts of healing due to His mood and the needs He desires to address in that session. But, in other gatherings, healing may not be mentioned at all, even though sick people may be present.

Determining the mood of the Holy Spirit in each meeting or situation helps to answer the question, What condition is God attempting to deal with? Going with the flow is always easier than going against it because the mood normally creates faith for things being taught, sung, or expressed.

Once the disposition of the Holy Spirit is determined, the third question must be posed to the Lord.

God, Is This Your Timing?

In this third step, the believer desiring to move in the gifts must decide if God is showing him something for the purpose of immediate action or for prayer, wisdom for counseling, or information to be used at a later time. It's not enough to simply get information from God. You have to have God's wisdom on what to do with it. Sometimes people make the mistake of taking a word from God that is for them personally and treating it as if it were given for everyone.

"Jesus," as the Bible says, *"knew all men"* and *"did not need man's testimony about man, for he knew what was in a man"* (John 2:24–25). Though Jesus knew by supernatural knowledge what was in the heart of every man, He did not feel compelled to declare something simply because He knew it. It was always a matter of God's timing and purpose. Jesus could have come immediately to heal Lazarus of his sickness, but He intentionally delayed because He knew the Father's plan. God's

plans are far more encompassing than what meets the eye. In Lazarus' case, God's glory increased through Jesus' delay (John 11:4), and Mary's and Martha's faith grew more.

Sometimes God will give you a prophetic word, not for the purpose of declaring it publicly, but to hide in your own heart. Then, when certain things come to pass, you will know that they are from the Lord.

In Saul's attempt to find his father's lost donkeys, his servant suggested that they go to the seer to inquire of God (1 Sam. 9:6, 9). As they came into the city, Samuel the prophet was about to go up to the high place to worship God.

> *Now the day before Saul came, the LORD had revealed this to Samuel: "About this time tomorrow I will send you a man from the land of Benjamin. Anoint him leader over my people Israel; he will deliver my people from the hand of the Philistines. I have looked upon my people, for their cry has reached me."* (vv. 15–16)

This biblical account helps to illustrate my point. Some things that are revealed will have meaning and relevancy at a later time. Although God gave Samuel a word of knowledge and a word of wisdom regarding the nation's future king, the application of the information did not follow until the next day.

A friend of mine shared with me a fascinating story of how his grandfather was used by God to work a miracle. His grandfather had been pastoring a small country church for several years when he became annoyed at his own passive, lukewarm Christian life. One day he started to bombard the heavens with earnest, heartfelt prayer that he and his church might be used by God to do something great. The Lord showed him a woman in his congregation who had suffered for years with an incurable disease, and God revealed to the pastor that He wanted to heal her. Encouraged by the revelation, the pastor quickly made an appointment to pray for the woman. However, when he prayed for her, nothing happened!

The pastor knew what God had shown him was accurate, but he had not yet received the revelation of how to bring it to pass. After twenty-one days of fasting and prayer about the situation, he made a second appointment with the woman. This time, as he laid his hands on her, a healing miracle took place right before his very eyes. Glory to God! The word of the Lord came to pass after he waited on God for special instructions. The Lord's timing was significant in this case.

God, Is This the Environment You Choose to Display Your Graciousness?

Environment refers to the setting, both spiritual and natural. Jesus preached in His hometown synagogue and astounded the people (Matt. 13:54–58). *"Where did this man get this wisdom and these miraculous powers?"* (v. 54), they said. Nevertheless, Jesus Himself could not do many miracles there because of the setting and the spiritual environment. In that case, some aspects of the natural environment, that is, the hometown where people were familiar with Jesus' family, created a spiritual environment that hindered the miraculous.

It would be erroneous to conclude that the right environment for the manifestation of the supernatural only occurs when you are surrounded by people who are friendly, supportive, and full of faith. That's not always the case. God's purpose is what matters most. One day you may be in what seems to be the worst situation possible. Nevertheless, this is often where God most wants to move.

One day a group of skeptical scribes and Pharisees showed up to hear Jesus teach. The biblical account reads, *"And the power of the Lord was present for him* [Jesus] *to heal the sick"* (Luke 5:17). Though the power was not present for a great number of miracles in His hometown, here it was the environment for something astonishing to happen.

It was on this occasion that a paralytic was let down on a stretcher through a hole in the roof. Jesus could have simply healed the man. But, being aware of the scribes and Pharisees looking on, probably with scowls on their faces, Jesus first said, *"Friend, your sins are forgiven"* (v. 20). It seems clear from the text that Jesus did this to intentionally provoke his religious detractors. It worked pretty well, too. They all began to argue against Him in their hearts, saying, *"Who is this fellow who speaks blasphemy? Who can forgive sins but God alone?"* (Luke 5:21).

Jesus replied to their inner thoughts, *"Which is easier: to say, 'Your sins are forgiven,' or to say, 'Get up and walk'?"* (v. 23). You know the rest of the story. The paralytic was healed, and, as a result, they were all seized with astonishment and began glorifying God.

It was easy for Jesus to say, *"Get up and walk,"* because it was an environment in which the power of the Lord was present to heal. The mere fact that the Scripture makes mention of the power of the Lord being present for Him to perform healing, enables us to infer that sometimes the power of the Lord is *not* present for healing. This further establishes my point. We need to consider the spiritual environment before we attempt to activate the gifts of the Spirit.

Several years ago I was asked to perform a eulogy at the funeral of one couple's infant daughter who had died of an illness. The baby's father, a New Jersey state trooper, had invited all of his fellow officers to the funeral. It was an extremely sad occasion, and the Christian parents were trying to reconcile in their minds God's love and their daughter's death. Even before the service began, I knew that this was going to be a tough one.

As I was bringing the eulogy to a close, I suddenly realized that the power of God was present to heal and deliver. I quickly ended my sermon, and right there at the funeral service I began operating in the gifts of the word of knowledge, the word of wisdom, faith, and the discerning of spirits. I'd never done anything like that before, nor had I heard of anyone else doing such a thing, and I certainly never expected what was about to happen. This was a funeral!

I remember distinctly walking out from behind the pulpit toward the congregation, picking out a woman, and giving her a powerful, encouraging word of knowledge. As I turned my back toward the congregation and began walking back to the pulpit, I heard these words in my spirit: "If you are a real man of God, pick me out, and give me a message from God." God had apparently enabled me, through the gift of the word of knowledge, to hear an internal thought of a person in the audience.

Immediately, I swung around and pointed to one of the state troopers sitting near the back, and I said, "Sir, you just said in your heart, 'If you are a real man of God, pick me out, and give me a message from God.' Stand in the aisle."

The officer in full dress uniform quickly stood in the aisle at the back with his hands by his side as I stood in the same aisle at the front. The scene was almost too incredible to believe. There I was, the minister at the funeral for a baby girl who had tragically passed away, in a sanctuary full of state troopers, and we were standing at opposite ends of the aisle like two gunfighters about to have a shoot-out.

I quickly dismissed the western imagery from my mind and proceeded to deliver an intense word of knowledge regarding the man's life and the recent thoughts of his heart.

Later, the father of the deceased infant told me what happened after the service. Out in the parking lot, his friend and fellow officer wanted to know how I knew all those things about him. I just chuckled to myself at the ways of God and the environment in which He chooses to display His power.

God, Am I the One You Wish to Use?

This is an extremely important question. Paul confronted Elymas the sorcerer and, by the gift of faith, voiced a miracle. Elymas was instantly blinded. Every Christian could not have done what Paul did, especially those having an immature mercy gift. This situation called for judgment, not for mercy. Furthermore, the individual with whom God chooses to co-labor has to be at a certain spiritual level. A person's maturity, both spiritual and natural, plays a major role in the things he can accomplish.

This is precisely why one must know the difference between revelation and application. What God is allowing you to see may not necessarily mean that you should try to do something about it. Much frustration can set in if you attempt to carry out in your flesh everything that God has shown you in your spirit.

A man came to Jesus with his son who was possessed by a demon. The demonic spirit had made the boy mute, and whenever it would seize him, he would stiffen, fall to the ground, foam at the mouth, and grind his teeth. The boy had been taken to Jesus' disciples, and even though they themselves were casting out many demons, they could not help this boy. After Jesus cast the demon out, His disciples asked why they could not cast it out. Jesus replied, *"This kind can come out only by prayer"* (Mark 9:29). Some manuscripts add the words, *"and fasting."*

The manifestation of the power of God required in this case was too great for the disciples without some serious prayer beforehand. The point is that there are varying degrees of spiritual challenges. Some believers are mature enough to meet them head-on, and others cannot do so without prayer, fasting, and, perhaps, a few more years of experience.

God, Is My Relationship with You at a Point Where I Can Actually Demonstrate Your Power with the Effectiveness This Situation Calls For?

In New Testament times, there were Jewish exorcists. One group of these exorcists were all sons of the Jewish chief priest. In *The New International Commentary on the New Testament,* F. F. Bruce says that a Jewish chief priest would enjoy high prestige in magical circles, for he was the sort of person most likely to know the true pronunciation of the Ineffable (unspeakable) Name of God.[3]

Having seen the power of God working through Paul, these exorcists decided they would try his methods; that is, they would say, *"In the name of Jesus, whom Paul preaches, I command you to come out"* (Acts 19:13). As these seven sons of Sceva were trying to cast out a demon this way, the demon said, *"Jesus I know, and I know about Paul, but who are you?"* (v. 15). The result was not good for the sons of Sceva.

> *Then the man who had the evil spirit jumped on them and overpowered them all. He gave them such a beating that they ran out of the house naked and bleeding.*　　　(v. 16)

The sons of Sceva were using the right words, but they didn't have the relationship with Jesus that would allow them to move in that kind of power and authority.

Recently, a woman came into one of our Sunday services with a very forlorn look on her face. I had never seen anyone so distraught in God's house, except in the midst of a funeral eulogy. Throughout the meeting, no semblance of joy or hope was reflected on her face.

Following the preaching of the Word, I felt impressed to minister to her. I called her forward, not knowing what to say, but assured in my heart that the God whom I serve is capable of meeting every need. A verse from one of the psalms of David rang in my heart: *"They* [children of men] *feast on the abundance of your house; you give them drink from your river of delights"* (Ps. 36:8). I knew God desired to give this woman a drink from the river of His delights.

As she stood at the front of the sanctuary, she exhibited some uneasiness, as if to say, "Why am I standing up here, and what do you want of me?" In a fraction of a second, the Lord spoke a word of knowledge to me. I looked intently at the woman and said the following to her: "You have attempted suicide several times, and you have considered killing your children. Furthermore, you have felt as if you were a prisoner behind bars, tormented by the thoughts of your mind. Today, God is going to free you from the bondage of darkness!"

As I was speaking, the woman began sobbing bitterly. I laid hands on her, and she went down under the power of God. When the two altar workers picked her up, her countenance had changed. She looked as if she had just been released from prison. Her face shone. I asked her if she wanted to accept Jesus Christ as her Savior and Lord. Without any hesitation, she emphatically said, "Yes!"

After I led her to the Lord, I gave her some instruction on receiving the baptism of the Holy Spirit, and I laid hands on her to administer the baptism. Again, she went down under the power of God, and this time she came up speaking in other tongues as the Spirit enabled her.

Several days later, one of the members of our fellowship came to me and said she had brought that woman to church. On the way home from Sunday's meeting, the woman told her she did not know how "that man" knew all those things about her, but it was all accurate. She said, "No one knew how I felt. I was a prisoner in my own body." As I listened to this tremendous testimony, I chuckled inwardly, because Jesus knew the woman's situation, and through the perspective of grace, she received "a gracious deliverance."

If I had not been in the right place of fellowship with God, He would not have instructed me to release the word of knowledge to the woman contemplating suicide. Just imagine if I had administered the word of knowledge incorrectly to her or embarrassed her publicly. A lawsuit would surely have followed! However, instead of legal action, deliverance resulted. Praise God!

The more you walk with God, the more He can trust and rely on you. What would have happened if Paul had not been in the proper place with God to call down blindness upon Elymas? He would have been the laughingstock of that city, and Sergius Paulus probably would not have been converted.

Ministering from the perspective of grace, unlike sovereignty, places a significant degree of responsibility upon the believer. Although the six-step process may seem lengthy, awkward, and unnatural, keep in mind that it only appears that way. When a strong, covenantal relationship is established with Christ, these questions and considerations are answered in the natural flow of your communion with the Holy Spirit. God said, *"Before they call I will answer; while they are still speaking I will hear"* (Isa. 65:24).

God knows His servant's desire before he even speaks it. Also, the closer you walk with the Father, the more apt you are to know His intentions before He speaks them. The dialogue, although it will have eternal ramifications, takes less than a split second to occur.

——Chapter 8——

Creating the Atmosphere for Spiritual Gifts

Creating the Atmosphere for Spiritual Gifts

Those who live according to the sinful nature
have their minds set on what that nature desires;
but those who live in accordance with the Spirit
have their minds set on what the Spirit desires.
—Romans 8:5

B elievers who wish to participate in the gifts of the Holy
Spirit must be conscious of daily cultivating three areas
in their lives: the environment of worship, the lifestyle
of faith, and carefulness to honor one another, which is a prin-
cipal ingredient in receiving blessings. These three areas are
essential elements in creating a suitable atmosphere for the
manifestation of the gifts of the Spirit. Note that this atmosphere must be established in two places: in the believer (the
temple of the Holy Spirit), and in the external surroundings
(the church, the conference setting, the home group, and so on).

External surroundings are important because the level of
faith (or the lack thereof) in a corporate gathering can influence
the manifestation of the gifts. Obviously, God can operate any-
where and in all sorts of environments. However, we are not
discussing an independent sovereign move, but the display of
the Spirit working in cooperation with a grace vessel. This is
considered a move of grace—God co-laboring with man.

The effectiveness of preaching and teaching is determined not only by the speaker preparing his heart and his mind, but also by things like the arrangement of the room, the meeting agenda, and the expectations of the audience. Distractions can easily kill a meeting no matter how effective the communicator is. Eyesores, uncomfortable conditions, interruptions, and uninterested people quench the flow of the Spirit because they take away from undistracted devotion directed toward the Lord. It is very similar to how you would feel if, in the middle of an intimate conversation with someone, you noticed that they weren't even paying attention. You would immediately close down the conversation. That's precisely how the Holy Spirit feels when He wants to share His heart with people who are not paying attention.

When we embark on the journey to understanding the charismatic gifts, issues such as the external atmosphere are very, very important. Just as other spiritual dynamics are affected by external things, so the manifestations of the gifts of the Spirit are thwarted by physical and spiritual realities.

The atmosphere where spiritual gifts flow freely is also affected by our expectations. When the gifts operate regularly in the church, people come with a sense of expectation. You don't have to over-advertise a meeting to get people excited, nor are they discouraged if nothing spectacular happens in a particular service. The levels of faith and expectation are cultivated over a long period of time.

In the same way, when there is never any expression of the gifts or the power of God in the church, it is often hard to overcome the long-term habit of low or no expectations. Just imagine reading an advertisement about a circus coming to town. In your excitement, you tell your children, and they tell a few of their close friends. Before you know it, you have a car loaded down with kids on the way to the circus. After paying the admission price at the gate, you go inside and are struck with the reality that things do not appear as they were advertised. None of the featured attractions mentioned on the flyer actually exist. It was only a ploy to get you to come—"bait and switch," they call it. How would you feel? What would you say to your children? The issue is not simply getting a refund; it becomes one of disappointment and unfulfilled expectations.

Every now and then we need to step back and evaluate what we as the church are saying to the world and how it appears in their eyes. We proclaim that God is in our midst, and we invite the world to come to church and meet Him. Many respond to the advertisement and arrive with great expectations. However, the power of their childlike faith cannot overcome a church full of people who are accustomed to expecting nothing. One of the first steps to activating the gifts of the Holy Spirit in the church is for the congregation to create the proper atmosphere. Let's explore this environment further.

THE ENVIRONMENT OF WORSHIP

Worship invokes gracious deliverances! Consequently, to facilitate the regularity of God's power, true worship must be present. When this occurs, we create an atmosphere where Christ is willingly enthroned. The Old Testament prophet Elisha, through whom the power gifts of the Holy Spirit were regularly demonstrated, provided for us an example of how worship prepares the way for the power of God to flow freely.

In the days of Elisha, Jehoram, the king of Israel, declared war on the neighboring country of Moab. The king of Moab had rebelled against Jehoram and had refused to pay tribute to Israel. Thus, Jehoram called on his allies, the king of Edom and the king of Judah, to go up together with him against Moab. On their way, however, all three armies ran out of water. In their desperate situation, Jehoshaphat, the king of Judah, suggested that they go to the home of Elisha the prophet to get a word from the Lord. The others agreed, and off they went. They were, however, not well received by Elisha, who was still angry over all that Jehoram's parents, King Ahab and Queen Jezebel, had done to his mentor, Elijah, and the nation of Israel.

"What do we have to do with each other?" Elisha said. *"Go to the prophets of your father and the prophets of your mother"* (2 Kings 3:13). Elisha's antagonism toward the king of Israel can really be interpreted, "What do we have in common?" or, rather, "What is it that has anything to do with both you and me?"

Elisha refused to listen to Jehoram. The prophet was so angry with Jehoram that he said, if it were not for the presence of

Jehoshaphat, he would not even have shown them his face. Nevertheless, out of respect for Jehoshaphat, Elisha finally agreed to prophesy over them, even though he was in no mood for it and did not even have a prophetic word to share.

The first thing that the angry prophet did was to create the environment in which the power of the Lord could be manifested. *"'But now bring me a harpist.' While the harpist was playing, the hand of the LORD came upon Elisha"* (2 Kings 3:15). Elisha must have known quite a bit about the spiritual realm, the gifts of the Spirit, and activities that entreat God to speak what is on His heart. The seasoned prophet asked for a harpist (or a minstrel, as it is found in the King James Version) to be brought to him so that he could have the right atmosphere for the move of the Spirit.

The New Strong's Complete Dictionary of Bible Words defines a minstrel as "one who beats a tune with the fingers; to play on a stringed instrument; to thrum."[1] This word is translated into the word *harpist* in the New International Version. Other Bible commentators use the word *flute-player*. Elisha's request for this specific type of person to be brought to him is more involved than one would think. He knew that the worshipful music played by the minstrel would quench his anger and still his heart to hear God.

Not every Christian musician understands God or knows how to cultivate an atmosphere of responsive worship. Merrill Unger, in *The New Unger's Bible Dictionary,* says of Elisha's request for a minstrel, "It may be that through the music he expected to 'collect his mind from the impressions of the outer world, and by subduing the self-life and life in the external world, to become absorbed in the intuition of divine things.'"[2]

When the musician was brought to Elisha, he probably played something soothing and worshipful, thereby creating an atmosphere for the reception and transmission of the prophetic word. The inspirational gift of prophecy was activated in Elisha as worship was embraced.

The effects of worship on the manifestation of the gifts and the power of God are not only found in this passage of Scripture; they are also located in several Old Testament accounts of prophets working miracles. (See 1 Samuel 10:5–7, for instance.)

David used his harp to help a demonized king with an evil spirit get control of himself (1 Sam. 16:16–17). True worship is a powerful force that by itself can alter lives and, in conjunction with a sensitive vessel, facilitate powerful acts of gracious deliverances.

When worship occurs in the internal sanctuary of one's heart, proper focus on God's agenda can take place. Worship is the creature's language of devotion and love for his Creator. It is the highest action of regard, respect, reverence, and homage one can pay to God. Voluntarily prostrating yourself before God in your heart, as well as with your body, entreats Him to speak, act, or perform His usual deeds of compassion and grace. Worship unlocks God's compassion.

There must be an environment of worship in both the external setting and the internal sanctuary of one's heart. A quality worship experience during corporate gatherings must first be born out of one's personal worship habits. In other words, if your lifestyle is one of worship, the atmosphere of worship is always created when you're around. In order to spark the faith and raise the level of expectancy of non-worshippers, an external worship environment must be established.

HONOR, A PRINCIPAL INGREDIENT

Recently a pastor friend of mine asked for my input on a spiritual dilemma he was facing. His church had just hosted a series of meetings in which a number of prophets were featured as guest ministers. This was not the first time his church had sponsored such a meeting. He noticed that, while the prophets were present in the church, he operated in the gifts of the Spirit alongside them. However, when the services ended and the prophets returned home, he no longer moved in the charismatic gifts. His question to me was, Why?

I quickly blurted out, "Honor is the issue! Your congregation views the visiting prophets as powerful men of God to whom they are looking for supernatural spiritual guidance and the manifestations of signs and wonders. Your ability to operate in spiritual gifts during their visit is because of the overflow of honor that touches you. When they return home, your parishioners cease to honor the vessels through whom God would like to move. They return to the former state of mind, thinking, 'Oh our pastor, he's such a nice man—very friendly. He's a good teacher, counselor, and administrator.' However, they don't give you credit or honor for being able to be used in the gifts. No honor, no expectancy—no manifestation."

The word *honor* means "high regard or great respect given or received; to treat with courtesy and respect." Honor, as it relates to manifesting spiritual gifts, is not talked about very much in the body of Christ. Notice that in the definition there is no indication of glory being distributed to men by other men, no flattery or patronizing. It clearly speaks of respect and implies admiration, esteem, consideration, reverence, and homage.

Glory is something entirely different. It is the deification of honor. God is the only one who should receive glory! As Jesus prayed, *"For thine is the kingdom, and the power, and the glory, for ever. Amen"* (Matt. 6:13 KJV).

Although God desires to be the sole object of man's adoration, He commands that we give honor to each other. *"Do nothing out of selfish ambition or vain conceit, but in humility consider others better than yourselves"* (Phil. 2:3). When we esteem our brothers and sisters, we essentially consider them better than ourselves. This is a primary aspect of honor.

Honoring the Holy Spirit in the Church

As I said in chapter six, the promise of the Father was that the Holy Spirit would be poured out on all flesh. Consequently, the gifts that demonstrate God's power and the prophetic ministry would be distributed throughout the church. In the Old Testament, there were a select few through whom the Spirit moved. In the New Testament, the Spirit displays that same prophetic ministry through the church, a "corporate man" made up of many members. Paul wrote about this very issue when he pointed out to the Ephesian church that the ministers of the body of Christ were given for this purpose:

[Ministers are given] *to prepare God's people for works of service, so that the body of Christ may be built up until we all reach unity in the faith and in the knowledge of the Son of*

God and become mature, attaining to the whole measure of the
fullness of Christ.   *(Eph. 4:12–13)*

The "mature man" who is in the fullness of Christ manifests all the gifts and character of God. However, God has not
purposed that the fullness should come through a few super-
Christians, but through the various members of the body. A few
verses later, Paul's words in the New American Standard Version read,

We are to grow up in all aspects into Him, who is the head,
even Christ, from whom the whole body, being fitted and held
together by that which every joint supplies, according to the
proper working of each individual part....   *(vv. 15–16)*

Since the gifts are distributed by the Holy Spirit throughout the body to each member, all parts have to function properly
for the full manifestation of the gifts to take place. That brings
me back to the issue of honor within the body. Paul listed the
nine gifts of the Spirit in 1 Corinthians 12:8–10. Right on the
heels of that discourse, he launched into an exhortation about
honoring the place and function of each member of the body.
Many people do not function in the spiritual gifts that the Holy
Spirit has distributed to them because they are too concerned
that others will look down on their bold step of faith. There are
those who might (and probably will) say, "Why, I know her. You
wouldn't believe all the problems she has! Who does she think
she is, prophesying like that?"

There are two problems with this situation. First of all, an
individual with a word from the Lord needs to obey God and
simply get over his or her concern of what others think. But
secondly, and probably more importantly, the body of Christ
needs to honor the gifts of God in all the members in order to
create an atmosphere where people can freely move in the gifts
of the Holy Spirit without feeling criticized and dishonored by
others. Since the gifts are to flow through the many-membered
body, honoring one another and the gifts that have been distributed to each member is a by-product of honoring the Holy
Spirit who is the distributor of such gifts.

There is nothing that will quench the flow of the spiritual gifts in a local congregation more than looking at one another critically and not recognizing the power of the Holy Spirit in each member. Those who are less confident about their gifts need to worship in an atmosphere where honor for one another exists, or they will seldom, if ever, step out. That's why Paul wrote,

> *Those parts of the body that seem to be weaker are indispensable, and the parts that we think are less honorable we treat with special honor....God has combined the members of the body and has given greater honor to the parts that lacked it.*
> *(1 Cor. 12:22–24)*

Paul was saying that those who are the least inclined to step out and move in the gifts of the Spirit need to be honored and encouraged the most.

The stumbling block of familiarity caused those in Nazareth to dishonor Jesus. The people of Nazareth, Jesus' hometown, were well acquainted with His family for many generations. So they refused to be instructed by Him. As a result of their blatant rejection, Jesus said to them, *"Only in his hometown, among his relatives and in his own house is a prophet without honor."* The passage goes on to say, *"He could not do any miracles there, except lay his hands on a few sick people and heal them"* (Mark 6:4–5). Even though the most anointed messenger of all was in their midst, they could not get over their familiarity to see Him as anything but a carpenter's son. How do you view your brothers and sisters in the body of Christ? Do you let the fact that you know them so well keep you from honoring the gifts that the Holy Spirit wants to manifest through them?

As Christ builds His church, much attention (unknown to many believers) is given to the ingredient of honor. In fact, the honor of the Lord must dwell in the church! The psalmist David wrote, *"LORD, I have loved the habitation of thy house, and the place where thine honour dwelleth"* (Ps. 26:8 KJV). When honor abides in the heart of each believer, the power of God is readily available. Conversely, where dishonor is present, very few miracles can occur.

Creating the Atmosphere for Spiritual Gifts

Honoring Those with Ministry Gifts

Not only are we to respect one another, but Scripture also commands us to honor our leaders:

> *Now we ask you, brothers, to respect those who work hard among you, who are over you in the Lord and who admonish you. Hold them in the highest regard in love because of their work.* (1 Thess. 5:12–13)

Pride is usually the reason why we don't esteem our brothers more highly than we do. Pride closes the door to honor, which is the inlet into the supernatural. Jesus said,

> *Anyone who receives a prophet because he is a prophet will receive a prophet's reward, and anyone who receives a righteous man because he is a righteous man will receive a righteous man's reward.* (Matt. 10:41)

I've heard it said that a prophet's reward is his prophecy. This means that when you honor a prophet of God, you're sure to see the manifestation of the Spirit of God. When you esteem a righteous man in the name of the Lord, you will receive a righteous man's reward: the knowledge of growing in the righteousness of Christ.

I recently preached a series of messages on spiritual authority at our church. It was a four-part teaching spanning a five-week period. In the third week, knowing a guest speaker was coming to our church, I focused on the subject of honoring those in ministry. This teaching prepared the people's hearts, awakening in them their responsibility to be courteous and respectful to the visiting minister. Everyone really went out of the way to show honor. The results were amazing!

This particular minister seldom moved in the gifts. We had had him at our fellowship once before, and not one manifestation was evidenced. But, prior to delivering his first sermon on this occasion, he began to minister powerfully through the gifts of the Spirit. The congregation literally drew out of him the blessings of God by creating an atmosphere of honor.

THE LIFESTYLE OF FAITH

Much has been taught about faith over the past twenty years. We have heard teachings on how to have faith in your faith, mountain-moving faith, the Thomas-kind of faith, and so forth. With all that instruction, the body of Christ has gained a lot of intellectual knowledge about faith. But, so often it has not resulted in experiential knowledge. I am convinced that the only way a person can really increase his or her faith level is through experience. No matter how much you are taught about faith, a gap always remains between knowing it and doing it.

Faith to operate in the gifts is no different from having faith for finances, for friends to be saved, or for marriages to be renewed. You have to step out of your comfort zone to see your prayers answered. How many people have you heard ask, "How do I know that God is speaking to me? Suppose I prophesy the wrong thing?" My response to such questions is, "Suppose you prophesy the right thing?" The only way to learn how to operate in the gifts is by doing it.

Obviously, some basic instructions are helpful, and so are a worship environment and a church that facilitates hearing from God and honors rather than criticizes. But faith is a muscle, and you have to use it in order for it to get stronger. When all is said and done, the only way you're going to move in the gifts is through the personal exercise of your faith.

One thing that stops people from utilizing faith is that their resources have not been fully depleted. When we have other options to explore before being at our wits' end, believing God by faith is not a viable alternative. Consequently, the demonstration of the gifts seldom occurs. I realized that this was the case early on in my Christian walk. The gifts were not being activated in my life because in my heart I was not yet ready to pay the price. Every spiritual growth spurt or step up to a higher rung on the growth ladder requires faith. True faith, however, can be equated with desperation. A person who is desperate is a person who has lost hope in anything and everything except his last option.

About a year into my Christian walk, I had become very desperate for God's power to be displayed in and through my life. I was tired of reading about it, hearing about it, and seeing it wonderfully displayed in the ministry of my pastor. However, that kind of power was not in my life.

My pastor moved in several different gifts of the Spirit so freely and regularly that I questioned whether they were genuine. I was discouraged by the dichotomy that I had allowed to dwell in my heart. One part of me wanted to see the supernatural expressions of the Holy Spirit. The other part of me tried to rationalize them away because, in truth, I was too lazy spiritually to climb to the next rung of the ladder through faith.

After several months of skeptical observation, my heart was drastically changed. The pastor ministered to me prophetically on issues that only God could have told him. After that, I was made a believer in the reality of the gifts of the Spirit. All of the ambivalence and double-mindedness ended that day, and I became desperate for God. True faith was born in my heart out of a need to see God's power operate in my life. I suddenly realized what Habakkuk felt when he cried, *"LORD, I have heard of your fame; I stand in awe of your deeds, O LORD. Renew them in our day, in our time make them known"* (Hab. 3:2). Habakkuk had become desperate for God's power to be demonstrated in his era and his life. My desperation made me vow to cry out to God every morning at 5:00 A.M. for the supernatural to be unlocked in my life.

It is amazing how God captures a person's heart, affection, devotion, and loyalty by choosing to be silent. When Moses went up to Mount Sinai to receive God's ordinances for the children of Israel, for the first six days God said absolutely nothing to him (Exod. 24:12–16). This must have seemed strange to Moses, because it was God who had summoned him in the first place. As I prayed each morning, the heavens seemed like brass; I felt as if God were nowhere to be found. This was His way of checking me out to see how serious I was for Him and how truly desperate I was for His gifts to operate through me. But I would not give up because I was desperate!

Finally, after several months, the gifts began to operate in my life. It happened at the close of a youth meeting. I had been invited one Friday night to speak to a few teenagers in a neighboring church. I was just twenty-one years old and had been a

Christian for one year. The youth minister thought I had something to say to his teens, so he invited me. I had never preached before, so I quickly concluded that I had nothing to lose.

That night I had only intended to share a few verses of Scripture. But, unbeknownst to me, God had much more in mind. As I was nervously bringing my message to a close, I heard certain words come into my mind—words that I knew did not originate from within my heart. It was a prophetic word from the Lord. I quickly shared it, and to my surprise, other information started to pour out of me like a river. The Lord was finally using me! Several gifts of the Spirit began operating that night. My desperation had paid off, and God rewarded my faith! All those months, when the heavens seemed like brass, were a time when in reality God was allowing my faith to grow. I learned something about God during that experience: in His silence He is always listening intently and never ignoring me.

Start off by asking God to speak small fragments of revelation knowledge to you, and then, over a period of time, aspire to "graduate" to weightier matters. For instance, pray that the unknown illnesses of people around you may be revealed to you by the Holy Spirit. Then progressively believe God that He will direct you to minister healing to one of these individuals. As you dare to believe God, He'll begin to use you to advance His kingdom.

In one's quest to receive the manifestation of the Spirit of God, it should be clear that God works in the framework of the local church. It is in this environment that the proper exercise of these gifts can be cultivated under church leadership. For this reason, Paul stated, *"Since you are eager to have spiritual gifts, try to excel in gifts that build up the church"* (1 Cor. 14:12).

Creating an environment in the local church for the Spirit of God to manifest Himself is quite exciting. God's power comes on the scene through grace when His sons and daughters take the personal responsibility to maintain a lifestyle consecrated to worship, faith, and honoring the presence of the Spirit in one another.

Maturity and Variety
of Spiritual Gifts

Maturity and Variety of Spiritual Gifts

*Now there are diversities of gifts, but the same
Spirit. And there are differences of administrations,
but the same Lord. And there are diversities of
operations, but it is the same God which
worketh all in all.*
—1 Corinthians 12:4–6 KJV

Walking with God is always exciting! As the Lover of our souls, He knows how to sustain the adventure in our relationship. Religious traditions can become boring and burdensome, but to those who follow Him closely, He continually brings forth a newness. And, since there is no end to His wonder, the Holy Spirit is forever teaching us how to view Him in a new light. Jeremiah described God's compassions by saying, *"They are new every morning"* (Lam. 3:23). God knows how to keep a good thing going!

After having escaped the sin and emptiness of a life without Christ, you will always be tempted to take it easy and camp out at some level of spiritual progress. This action is similar to that of the children of Israel, who crossed the Jordan, inhabited most of the Promised Land, but became complacent and did not occupy it fully. God wants you to get out of your comfort zone and allow Him to reveal Himself to and through you in varying ways. He also wants you to move up to higher, more mature expressions of the gifts.

When Paul exhorted the Corinthian church to *"eagerly desire spiritual gifts"* (1 Cor. 14:1), it was in the context of moving ahead—from giving a message in tongues without an interpretation to giving a prophecy. We are to press on in spiritual maturity and develop our ability to minister to the body in more effective ways. Your past spiritual accomplishments have not begun to exhaust your potential in God.

FLEEING BOREDOM

How many ways can the Holy Spirit express the nine gifts through the members of the body? The possibilities are endless. I want to discuss a few ways of drawing out the vast amount of latent manifestations in the body of Christ. Our motive for eagerly desiring spiritual gifts should be, of course, to build up the body of Christ, not to bring attention to ourselves. Focusing on Christ and the purposes of His kingdom is the character of spiritual maturity, as well as the prerequisite for moving in deeper levels of spiritual manifestations.

My desire to move in varied expressions of the Holy Spirit first became a conscious thought when the church I pastor started showing signs of disinterest when I operated in the gifts. For some, it was over a period of months; for others, it had taken years. As a whole, the congregation's enthusiasm had been gradually declining for some time.

The meetings were not boring to visitors or to the most recent members. Gifts such as prophecy, words of knowledge and wisdom, faith, discerning of spirits, and gifts of healings were normally operative. The problem was that most of the long-standing members were so used to seeing the same gifts being manifested in the same ways that they were no longer applying their faith during the time of personal ministry to others.

After a person becomes familiar with something, no matter how spectacular, bizarre, or intriguing, he tends to lose interest. The average New Yorker becomes numb to the daily antics of some of the street peddlers and homeless people he sees every day. Long-term residents are no longer moved by the weirdness that is evident in their city. However, if an out-of-towner visits New York, he is most likely going to be shocked by what he sees.

I had a dilemma. What was I to do with a church that loves to see people receive deliverance through the supernatural but had become bored as a result of seeing the same regular displays of the gifts? I had three choices. I could say to the congregation, "God only uses me this way. I can't be anything different!" I could keep my mouth shut and resist my inclination to move in the gifts of the Holy Spirit. Or, thirdly, I could search the Scriptures for antidotes and pray for specific instructions from God. I chose to go with the last option—to search the treasure chest of God's Word and to pray.

As I sought God, He reminded me of the marriage covenant and the shared responsibility of each partner to maintain a mutually satisfying level of excitement and fulfillment in the relationship. By comparing the marriage covenant to my covenant with God, I suddenly realized that it was my responsibility to become more creative in the flow of the gifts. I was to instruct the congregation on how to create an atmosphere of excitement so that our covenantal community would receive maximum fulfillment.

Out of this encounter with the Lord, I began to understand the potential of each of the gifts. With a fresh scriptural outlook on the spiritual gifts, I began praying fervently for God to birth within me a capacity and an understanding of how to operate in deeper and varied levels of the gifts already functioning in my life.

One of the gifts in which God frequently uses me is the word of knowledge. It has already been stated that this gift unveils God's knowledge regarding a person, place, thing, feeling, or idea in the past or present. Normally, when I would operate in this gift, God would speak fragments of information to me about someone. However, since being challenged by God and His people to broaden my expectations, I now experience about ten different forms of manifestation of this one gift.

VARYING EXPRESSIONS OF THE GIFTS

God's essence and nature never change. They represent the established structure of His character, His behavior, His mannerisms. Nevertheless, He enjoys displaying His love and His intentions in new styles. When it comes to the manifestation of the Spirit, there is no exception—the Father enjoys a variety of expressions.

From the beginning, a diversity in the operation of the gifts has existed. The discussion on the operation of the gifts contained in chapter six should have made it clear that each gift has distinctly different and unique functions. However, the variety of expressions that I am referring to is a variation in the manifestation of each gift with regard to its form and depth of expression. The nine gifts can be displayed in various forms of appearance and operation. Consequently, I refer to them as nine *groups* of gifts.

The apostle Paul introduced the passage listing the nine gifts by saying,

> *Now there are diversities of gifts, but the same Spirit. And there are differences of administrations, but the same Lord. And there are diversities of operations, but it is the same God which worketh all in all.* (1 Cor. 12:4–6 KJV)

In other words, each gift can be exhibited by the Spirit in various ways and levels of maturity through each person. The use of the words *diversities* and *differences* in this passage implies that it was God's intention from the beginning to establish the gifts with varied depths. Most Christians don't realize this because they are still struggling with the basic issue of how to flow in the gifts.

This discussion of deeper levels of supernatural manifestations is primarily for those who have already learned how to move in the gifts and are now interested in exploring the potential of the diversities of gifts, differences in administrations, and diversities of operations. The topic being discussed here, then, is how an individual can receive a variety of manifestations within the same gift.

DIVERSITIES OF GIFTS

The term *"diversities of gifts"* refers to the distinctive varieties of supernatural expressions of the Holy Spirit. There are many gifts, yet *"the same Spirit"* is the only source empowering the various manifestations. The church is a "uni-versity" in the truest sense of the word. There is a diversity of gifts, but they are unified by a common source and purpose.

Noted New Testament professor Dr. Gordon Fee points out in *The New International Commentary on the New Testament* that Paul's clear intent was to show that there are various gifts originating from the same Spirit because it is in keeping with the character of God. "The one God," Fee writes, "who is Himself characterized by diversity within unity, has decreed the same for His church."[1] He goes on to say that connecting the diversity of the gifts, administrations, and operations to the same Spirit, Lord, and God is a reference to the Trinity. In short, why are the gifts so varied and dispersed? It is because the church is to be a reflection of what God is like.

Paul's discussion of the gifts in 1 Corinthians should not be taken out of its original context. In chapters twelve through fourteen of 1 Corinthians, Paul explained that distinct and specialized giftings work through a unified group of people who all recognize the importance of each and every functioning part.

It's not unlike a great basketball team. Every team member can dribble, shoot free throws, play defense, pass, and rebound. But, in addition to those common giftings, there are specializations. Point guards dribble and pass especially well. Centers and power forwards play the inside game under the basket. Quick, little guys never make good centers, and a seven-footer would never make it as a point guard.

The key to a great team is, first of all, every player understanding his gifts and his roles. Secondly and equally important is that the players have to work together and coordinate their efforts. A "ball hog" who thinks he is "the answer" can turn a championship contender into a mediocre team that never gets above the middle of the pack.

Just like a basketball team, all the members of the body of Christ can move in many of the gifts to a certain degree. Yet, the Holy Spirit wants to perfect and mature some of those gifts in a person in order to establish that person's function and ministry in the church. This is synonymous to perfecting the art of dribbling and passing in order to function well as a point guard.

We also must learn to work together so that our ministries complement each other. One who gives a message in tongues is complemented by the one who has the interpretation. One who has the word of knowledge about a physical problem in someone's life is complemented by the person with the gifts of faith and healing.

The nine gifts of the Spirit listed in 1 Corinthians 12 also work in conjunction with the motivational gifts of Romans 12:6–8 and the ministry gifts of Ephesians 4:11. One in whom the word of knowledge is highly developed may be used to identify dark, hidden secrets that have been tormenting a person's life for years. Yet, the one with the word of knowledge may be totally unequipped to minister to that person through weeks and months of counseling in order to see him completely restored. Consequently, the Holy Spirit passes the ball to people with the gifts of mercy and wisdom who serve as pastors and counselors.

In conjunction with the interrelated nature of spiritual gifts, God also allows a variety of specializations to operate in and through each vessel. For example, invariably when I am ministering to someone, I can detect through the gift of discerning of spirits or the word of knowledge if that person is suicidal. God has enhanced this particular manifestation of His Spirit in my life, so that a specialized expression of the gifts occurs. However, I don't experience the Spirit's insights or manifestations when I deal with people who have psychological problems.

I know of other Christians operating in the gifts who have a tendency to spot emotional and psychological disorders in people. The Spirit's manifestation in their ministries results in the total deliverance of the people to whom they minister. However, those who can supernaturally detect signs of emotional problems don't necessarily experience the Holy Spirit's leading or power, as I do, when it comes to suicidal tendencies. God, in His infinite wisdom, causes the body of Christ to be interdependent, even in the specialization of spiritual gifts. That's the way the gifts of the Spirit are supposed to work in the body of Christ!

Maturity and Variety of Spiritual Gifts

Maturity and Intensity of a Gift

Within the context of each group of gifts, there are varying levels of intensity, depending on the maturity of the vessel through whom the gift flows. Praying in tongues is a common experience for those who first receive the baptism in the Holy Spirit. Though praying in tongues is very common, messages to the church in a tongue coupled with an interpretation don't happen as frequently. I've never personally experienced it, but I have heard accounts of people speaking or praying in tongues that were unknown to them but understandable to those who overheard. This more dramatic and intense manifestation is essentially what happened on the Day of Pentecost. The disciples spoke in the languages of those who were visitors in Jerusalem. The gift, in that instance, was manifested in a unique way for a sign to unbelievers.

It's one thing to prophesy to a person, saying simply that God loves him and has a plan for his life. This may, indeed, be the perfect timing and the exact message they need to hear from God. It is another thing, however, to give a prophecy that publicly and specifically reveals the secrets of a person's heart, even hidden sin, as it was in the case of Peter and his revelation about Ananias and Sapphira (Acts 5:1–10). For the more intense manifestation, a higher level of maturity and understanding of the operations of the gifts is required.

A gift of healing can be manifested when the elders come together to anoint a sick person with oil, lay their hands on the person, and pray. However, it was a much more mature expression of the power of God when famed evangelist Smith Wigglesworth prayed for a woman who was so weak and close to death that she could scarcely even lift her finger. The woman actually died even as he and one of the elders prayed for her. Wigglesworth pulled her out of bed, dragged her across the room, and stood her up against the wall. He rebuked death and commanded her to walk in the name of Jesus. The woman was completely restored and came to a public meeting with her doctor to testify to the fact.

It would be a mistake for a young Christian or one inexperienced in the gifts of healing or working of miracles to presume that he should do likewise simply because it worked for Wigglesworth. Stanley Frodsham's *Smith Wigglesworth, The Apostle of Faith,* says that the Spirit moved the evangelist to such a bold action because the gifts had been developed and matured to that point in his life.[2]

Unique Expressions of a Gift

Having a manifestation that differs entirely in appearance from the way someone else flows in the same gift is not altogether unusual. As previously mentioned, the gifts operate through the personality of the user. They are an act of grace in which the Holy Spirit co-labors with the members of the body. The co-laboring causes each gift to have a unique expression. You might say that a gift of the Holy Spirit is "flavored" by the uniqueness and maturity of the vessel. The motivational gifts of Romans 12:6–8 (mercy, teaching, giving, and so on) may differ greatly from person to person. Therefore, the expressions of the spiritual gifts (1 Cor. 12) through each individual are uniquely shaped by the personality and the motivational gifts within a person.

When someone prophesies via the gift of prophecy, according to Scripture, that prophecy is designed to strengthen, encourage, and comfort the hearer (1 Cor. 14:3). Judging from the vastness of personality types, cultures, races, and educational levels in the body of Christ, a single style of delivery of a prophetic word is not sufficient to provide gracious deliverances for everyone. Therefore, God in His omniscience provided diversities of expressions to meet every need.

DIFFERENCES OF ADMINISTRATIONS

The term *"differences of administrations"* (1 Cor. 12:5 KJV) refers to the office or official service associated with the manifestation of each gift. In order to get a better grasp of this issue, one should realize that the phrase being analyzed is connected to the word *Lord: "And there are differences of administrations, but the same Lord"* (v. 5 KJV). The word *Lord* is the Greek word *kurios,* which means "supreme in authority; controller or master." The idea Paul was conveying here is that there are varied levels of authority that operate with each manifestation. Also, there is order to everything that God establishes. Order is necessary to avoid chaos, confusion, and error.

One part of the vision God has given me for our local church is to believe Him for a prophetic orchestra. This encompasses skilled singers and musicians who are also capable of singing and playing the song of the Lord. The term *song of the Lord* means the unrehearsed, spontaneous release of a spiritual song (with or without music) to the church or to God.

To adequately train our worship team (singers and musicians) to move in the dimension of the song of the Lord, God graciously allows me to operate at a higher administrative level of the word of knowledge than the worship team. Training people to move in spiritual things is not always easy. The teacher must be well versed in the subject matter and also know where the students are spiritually.

I find that many people hesitate to operate in the gifts because they are afraid of missing God. To help alleviate the fear among our worship leaders, God allows me to actually hear the song of the Lord before it is sung by a singer. When I hear the song, I normally say, "I hear the song of the Lord. Bring it forth." The one who has the song and has been reluctant to share it gains confidence and ministers the song because of my confirmation.

There are times following my statement when no one shares a prophetic song. The Lord then directs me to go over to the person quenching the song and say, "Release the song of the Lord." The person usually smiles, as if to say, "How did you know I had the song?" He can then easily release the song. I have noticed that as our worship leaders mature spiritually and gain confidence in God, the Lord lets me hear the songs on fewer occasions.

Differences of administrations in the gifts is one of God's ways of bringing order to the supernatural display of His Spirit. As Samuel stood over the prophets, judging the accuracy of their prophecies and mannerisms, the authority delegated to him by God was clearly evident (1 Sam. 19:20). He had to move in an administrative level of the gifts with which he was endowed in order to properly critique the prophets he was training.

In 1 Corinthians 14, Paul continued his exhortation on spiritual gifts:

> *Two or three prophets should speak, and the others should weigh carefully what is said. And if a revelation comes to someone who is sitting down, the first speaker should stop. For you can all prophesy in turn so that everyone may be instructed and encouraged. The spirits of prophets are subject to the control of prophets. For God is not a God of disorder but of peace.* *(1 Cor. 14:29–33)*

There is spontaneity in a service where the gifts of the Holy Spirit are allowed to flow freely, but there is also an order. Judging the accuracy of prophetic words is not a democratic process accomplished by popular vote. The implication of the text is that judging prophetic utterances is to be done by mature, proven prophetic ministers in the church. The same prophetic gift resides in many people throughout the church, but still there are *"differences of administrations"* regarding their office and authority.

In some churches, prophetic utterances, words of knowledge, and so on, are given spontaneously by people in the congregation. In other churches, people come to the front and share their revelation with elders and prophetic ministers. Then, at the right time in the service, the leaders bring forth various individuals who have something from the Lord to share with the body. Sometimes several people receive the same or similar revelation independently. That is the Holy Spirit's way of confirming what He wants to say. In *Growing in the Prophetic,* Mike Bickle says that some pastors like to have directional words for the church or the worship service confirmed by several prophetic words before they will share it or radically change the direction the service.[3]

However the gifts of the Spirit are handled in a particular church, the goal is that there is an administration of the gifts which enables the Spirit to move through the members and at the same time allows for all things to be done in order. Without this ministry of administration, things get out of order and, in our effort to give room for the Spirit to move, we actually wind up quenching the Spirit.

DIVERSITIES OF OPERATIONS

The third issue relating to the variety of expressions of the gifts is found in 1 Corinthians 12:6: *"And there are diversities of operations, but it is the same God which worketh all in all"* (KJV). The Amplified Bible reads, *"And there are distinctive varieties of operation* [of working to accomplish things], *but it is the same God Who inspires and energizes them all in all."* This passage of Scripture clearly indicates that God personally inspires distinctive varieties of manifestations to accomplish a vast array of tasks.

The point here is that God will accomplish the same thing in a variety of ways. If the Holy Spirit wants to point out that there is a person with a spinal injury or abnormality that He desires to heal, He might reveal it in one of several ways. One person might have a vision of the spinal problem. Another might feel a pain or a burning sensation in his spine and realize it is the Spirit revealing something to him. Another person might simply get a word of knowledge. The Holy Spirit might reveal the problem in all of the above ways or just to one person. In any case, the Holy Spirit accomplishes the same purpose through diversities of operations.

Isn't this trait characteristic of a Father who has many children? Knowing that different predicaments require different tactics and rescue efforts, the Lord allows diversities of operations to take place in the gifts.

SPIRITUAL GIFTS AND THE FIVE SENSES

There are many examples of spiritual gifts and communications being perceived by the physical senses. John saw the Holy Spirit descending upon Jesus in the form of a dove. On the Day of Pentecost, people saw tongues of fire and heard a noise like a mighty, rushing wind. As I mentioned earlier, some people receive a word of knowledge about spiritual as well as physical problems, in the form of physical pain or sensations.

On the road to Damascus, Paul ran into the risen Lord Jesus Christ.

> *Suddenly a light from heaven flashed around him. He fell to the ground and heard a voice say to him, "Saul, Saul, why do you persecute me?"...The men traveling with Saul stood there speechless; they heard the sound but did not see anyone.*
>
> *(Acts 9:3–4, 7)*

The point here is that the spiritual realm is not less real, but more real than the physical world. However, those in the flesh are only able to see the realities of the spirit realm when God opens their eyes.

Sometimes when a person is filled with or "caught up in" the Spirit, the spiritual world becomes so real in his perception that it is hard for him to tell whether he is seeing, feeling, or hearing with physical or spiritual senses. Paul wrote about such an event.

> *I know a man in Christ who fourteen years ago was caught up to the third heaven. Whether it was in the body or out of the body I do not know—God knows. And I know that this man— whether in the body or apart from the body I do not know, but God knows—was caught up to paradise. He heard inexpressible things, things that man is not permitted to tell.*
>
> *(2 Cor. 12:2–4)*

Spiritual realities that are experienced with the five senses are, in many ways, more intense than other experiences, though they are not necessarily a mark of maturity. Sometimes the physical-sense manifestations are due to spiritual immaturity and insensitivity. For example, God moved in a very visible way to Pharaoh because of the hardness of his heart. Also, the prophetic word of judgment came to Belshazzar in the form of a hand writing on the wall (Dan. 5).

Do you remember the story about God calling Moses, Aaron, and Miriam out to the Tent of Meeting to rebuke Aaron and Miriam for the way they were gossiping about Moses? God's statement to them also points to the reality of administrative levels of spiritual gifts. He said,

Listen to my words: "When a prophet of the LORD is among you, I reveal myself to him in visions, I speak to him in dreams. But this is not true of my servant Moses; he is faithful in all my house. With him I speak face to face, clearly and not in riddles."   *(Num. 12:6–8)*

Apparently, God views verbal communication on a higher order than receiving dreams or visions. This brings us to the conclusion that verbal dialogue reflects more intimacy than other forms of communication.

Elisha knew that the power of God surrounded him, but he prayed for the eyes of his servant to be opened, to calm his fears. *"Then the LORD opened the servant's eyes, and he looked and saw the hills full of horses and chariots of fire all around Elisha"* (2 Kings 6:17).

In order for the Holy Spirit to flow freely in our midst, we have to rid ourselves of dogmatic preconceptions of exactly how the Holy Spirit will or will not manifest His presence and power. His expressions and operations can be as diverse as the personalities and giftings of the members of the body of Christ. At the same time, every doctrinal position or spiritual activity one embraces must have its roots in the Bible. All manifestations must be discerned and judged by the Word of God. They must either have specific biblical precedent or be consistent with the character of the Holy Spirit as revealed in Scripture. As leaders continue to emerge and mature in the gift of administration with regard to the gifts, the Holy Spirit will move in our midst with more and more diversity.

——Chapter 10——

How to Activate
the Spiritual Gifts

—*Chapter 10*—

How to Activate
the Spiritual Gifts

*Therefore everyone who hears these words of mine
and puts them into practice is like a wise man
who built his house on the rock....
But everyone who hears these words of mine
and does not put them into practice is like a
foolish man who built his house on sand.*
—*Matthew 7:24, 26*

It was never my intention to simply write one more book explaining the charismatic gifts. One of my most important life objectives is to enable people to activate the gifts of the Holy Spirit in their lives. It's something I'm passionate about because, first of all, I know that the grace of God has already been made available, and, secondly, I know what can happen when people begin to co-labor with the Holy Spirit. I sincerely hope you don't just put this book down and continue your daily spiritual routine, because you can be a dynamic agent in the hands of God!

Though we commonly use the term *step of faith,* the phrase, as such, is not found in the New Testament. Perhaps the idea that an expression of faith is sometimes a "step of uncertainty" originated with the story of Peter walking on the water. The disciples, who were astonished to see Jesus walking on the sea,

165

were perhaps even more astonished when He bid Peter to come to Him by walking on the water himself.

When you think about it, Peter stepping out of the boat onto the raging sea was one of the greatest miracles of the New Testament. Oh, yes, there was the feeding of the five thousand, the raising of Lazarus, and the calming of the storm. But these were things that Jesus did alone, by His own authority. Philip the evangelist was miraculously transported by the Spirit after baptizing the Ethiopian eunuch, but that was a sovereign act, something that simply happened to him without any cooperation on his part.

What happened to Peter on the Sea of Galilee that night is an example of God's power working with and through a man's faith. Peter, the impulsive fisherman, stepped out in faith and walked on water! It is obvious that it was Jesus who was the essential element of the miracle, but what more amazing thing has any man ever done?

God wants to work in and through His people, including you. However, it's probably not going to happen in a sovereign act as it did with Philip. That kind of manifestation is extremely rare. Nor is God going to work miracles without using human instruments. God wants to reveal His power and His presence by co-laboring with us. Just as it was with Peter, that kind of miracle takes place only when we take the perilous leap of faith.

To co-labor with God, we have to be *"doers of the word, and not hearers only"* (James 1:22 KJV). Another way to put it is, we have to be steppers and not sitters. So then, I want to propose a plan of action, some practical steps you can take that will help you to start the process of walking in the manifestations of the gifts of the Holy Spirit.

SET YOUR HEART ON SEEKING THE LORD

You've probably heard it said that prayer doesn't change God, it changes us. That is indeed true, and what often changes is our will, desire, and agenda. Spending quality time with God brings you to the place where you say, "Not my will, but thine be done." Jesus Himself taught us to pray in this way: *"Thy kingdom come. Thy will be done in earth, as it is in heaven"*

(Matt. 6:10 KJV). Those who only come to God with shopping list in hand will eventually be disillusioned. "Why, I've prayed for months," they may say, "and I have gotten no answer! God must have forsaken me!"

The reason for their disappointment could be that their approach to God (with wish list always in hand) has kept them just as centered on their own will and their own agenda as when they began. The point of prayer is to abide in Him and to make His will and agenda your own. This kind of friendship and communion with God is the key to moving in the gifts of the Spirit.

BAPTIZE YOURSELF IN THE WORD OF GOD

Jesus said, *"If ye abide in me, and my words abide in you, ye shall ask what ye will, and it shall be done unto you"* (John 15:7 KJV). When God's Word abides in your heart (not just in your mind), it increases your discernment and your ability to think God's thoughts along with Him. Reading and meditating on the Scriptures enlightens and renews your mind and feeds your spirit. Paul's prayer for the Ephesians was the following:

> [God] *may give you the Spirit of wisdom and revelation, so that you may know him better. I pray also that the eyes of your heart may be enlightened in order that you may know the hope to which he has called you, the riches of his glorious inheritance in the saints, and his incomparably great power for us who believe.* (Eph. 1:17–19)

Spiritual power comes, in part, as a result of the revelation knowledge of who God is, of your inheritance as a joint-heir with Christ, and of the surpassing greatness of His power available to you. That revelation knowledge comes from spending time in God's Word with the Holy Spirit as your tutor.

RECOGNIZE THE HOLY SPIRIT

James said that one of the reasons why we do not receive is that we do not ask (James 4:2). In the same way, we often do not experience the presence, power, or direction of the Spirit because we do not recognize His presence in our lives. If you ignore the Spirit of God, He probably won't scream at you. There are so many opportunities missed, not because people are so extraordinarily hard of hearing, but because they are just not paying attention. Learn by practice to listen expectantly and continually to the Holy Spirit. You may be surprised to find out that He has been there all along, wanting to use you and ready to help you. He has been waiting for you to tune in.

BECOME AN INTERCESSOR
ON THE WAY TO BEING AN INSTRUMENT

Learning how to let the Holy Spirit flow through you should begin by letting Him flow through you in prayer and intercession. The ministry of the Holy Spirit praying through us is described in Paul's letter to the Romans:

> *The Spirit helps us in our weakness. We do not know what we ought to pray for, but the Spirit himself intercedes for us with groans that words cannot express. And he who searches our hearts knows the mind of the Spirit, because the Spirit intercedes for the saints in accordance with God's will.*
>
> *(Rom. 8:26–27)*

Faith is like a muscle, and exercising spiritual gifts only enables you to grow stronger. A greater and more accurate sense of discernment also comes through practice (Heb. 5:14). Jude's epistle says, *"But you, dear friends, build yourselves up in your most holy faith and pray in the Holy Spirit"* (Jude 1:20).

A person who regularly stands before God on behalf of other people will be enabled to stand before other people on behalf of God. Ezekiel prophesied, *"I* [God] *looked for a man among them who would build up the wall and stand before me in the gap on behalf of the land so I would not have to destroy it, but I found none"* (Ezek. 22:30). That had not always been the case. Moses was one who had "stood in the gap" for God's people. In a psalm recalling the history of Israel, David wrote,

So he [God] *said he would destroy them—had not Moses, his chosen one, stood in the breach before him to keep his wrath from destroying them.* (Ps. 106:23)

No other man has ever heard from and spoken for God as Moses did. But he did so because he was willing to be an intercessor.

PERFECT AND PROVE YOUR SERVE

Sometimes people desiring to move in the gifts of the Spirit are surprised when they realize that they are viewed with a degree of suspicion. They don't understand why the pastors, leaders, and others in the church are not more excited about their gifts. However, good leaders always get around to asking questions about the motivation of a person's heart. "What's driving their desire to move in the gifts?" they wonder. "Does it come from a long-term commitment to serve the church and the people? Is this about establishing the kingdom and building up the church, or is it about establishing their personal ministry and building up their reputation?"

If you can't identify or understand that kind of questioning, you've never felt the heart of a pastor. In fact, one of the charges to elders is to protect the flock from people who are not committed to building the local church (Acts 20:28–31).

Manifestations of spiritual gifts that are most easily received by the church leadership are the ones that come from people who have served the church in ways that demonstrate that their heart is for the well-being of the local body. In a sense, you earn that trust by becoming a person who has made a great investment in the church. If you're new in a church or if you've never been involved in the things that make the church function, ask God how you can serve in practical ways. God Himself may test the level of commitment and willingness to serve His church by leading a person with a strong prophetic gifting to volunteer to help set up chairs or clean the restrooms.

FIND A MENTOR

The best and quickest way to grow is to get around a person or persons who are mature in the operation of the gifts. In the

Old Testament, references are made to the *"sons of the prophets"* (2 Kings 6:1 KJV) and the *"company of the prophets"* (1 Sam. 19:20 KJV). Presumably, there was some kind of mentoring program to train younger men who had prophetic callings.

Some churches have small groups that meet for the purpose of exercising and maturing in the gifts of the Spirit. Other churches have mature pastors who are responsible for leading people who have a ministry of moving in spiritual gifts. These are not available in every church, but all of these ministries started somewhere, usually when people would get together to encourage and pray for one another. Some of the greatest spiritual growth environments are in groups where people simply get together for prayer and to hold each other accountable.

BE PATIENT AND PERSISTENT

The writer of Hebrews wrote of mature believers, *"who by constant use have trained themselves to distinguish good from evil"* (Heb. 5:14). I played baseball in college, and I played semi-pro for a few years. It was pretty scary the first time I ever saw a ninety-mile-per-hour fastball. But with practice—a *lot* of practice—what seemed impossible at first was not so overwhelming. It just takes getting your senses and reflexes trained so that you can hit the ball.

I've seen a lot of athletes get off to a phenomenal start, and, as a result, they were compared to the greatest players of all time in their early days. So often all the pressure that came along with the attention and notoriety killed their future. Similarly, on many occasions there have been people who have been used by the Spirit to bring about one significant miracle. Then they spend the next ten years on the speaking circuit telling about it.

But the gifts of the Spirit should flow out of an ongoing relationship with the Holy Spirit. God is not interested in making you a celebrity at the cost of His relationship with you. Be persistent in all the practical things I've mentioned above, but be patient, too. God will indeed manifest the gifts He has placed in you. Don't worry about stumbling along the way or times when you missed the mark. And don't be concerned about obscurity or what others think. God will allow the gifts in you to be recognized and esteemed in His perfect timing.

The issue of the gifts of the Spirit can easily become a theological debate or a philosophical argument. However, when the reality of broken, shattered lives begins to affect your comfort zone, the power of God available through the gifts of the Spirit will become something you covet. The following words of conviction, penned by Frances Roberts, encapsulate this thought.

LAUNCH OUT!

Thus saith the Lord unto His people:
Lo, ye have touched only the fringes.
Yea, thou hast lingered upon the shore lines.
Launch out, yea, launch out upon the vast bosom of My love
    and mercy, yea, My mighty power and limitless resources.
For lo, if thou wouldst enter into all that I have for thee, thou
    must walk by faith upon the waters.
Thou must relinquish forever thy doubts; and thy thoughts of
    self-preservation thou must forever cast aside.
For I will carry thee, and I will sustain thee by My power in the
    ways that I have chosen and prepared for thee.
Thou shalt not take even the first step in thine own strength.
For thou art not able in thyself—even as flesh is ever unable to
    walk the way of the Spirit.
But mine arm shall uphold thee, and the power of My Spirit
    shall bear thee up.
…Be not fearful but believing.[1]

Begin seeking His face right now! Cultivate an attitude of willingness and expectancy. The Holy Spirit wants to co-labor with you through grace. Don't put off stepping out in faith any longer by waiting for God to sovereignly move. Grace to co-labor with the Holy Spirit is waiting for you!

Endnotes

Chapter 1: Natural Enemies of Spiritual Gifts

[1] Carroll E. Simcox, *4400 Quotations for Christian Communicators* (Grand Rapids: Baker, 1991), 138.

[2] *The Interpreter's Bible,* vol. VIII (Nashville: Abingdon, 1952), 204.

[3] Norval Geldenhuys, *The New International Commentary on the New Testament, The Gospel of Luke* (Grand Rapids: Eerdmans, 1988), 326.

[4] Donald Palmer, *Looking at Philosophy* (Mountain View, CA: Mayfield, 1988), 57–58.

[5] William DeArteaga, *Quenching the Spirit* (Lake Mary, FL: Creation House, 1992), 74–77.

[6] George Barna, *What Americans Believe* (Ventura, CA: Regal, 1991), 204.

[7] Jack Deere, *Surprised by the Power of the Spirit* (Grand Rapids: Zondervan, 1993), 267.

[8] DeArteaga, *Quenching the Spirit,* 67–70.

[9] Rudolf Bultmann, *Kerygma and Myth.* Ed. H. W. Bartsch. Trans. Reginald M. Fuller (New York: Harper & Row, 1961), 291–292.

[10] *Eerdmans' Handbook to the History of Christianity* (Grand Rapids: Eerdmans, 1977), 598–599.

[11] C. S. Lewis, *Miracles* (New York: Macmillan, 1947), 105.

[12] G. Curtis Jones, *1000 Illustrations for Preaching and Teaching* (Nashville: Broadman, 1986), 234.

Chapter 2: Sovereignty and God's Calling

[1] W. E. Vine, *An Expository Dictionary of New Testament Words* (Iowa Falls, IA: Riverside Book and Bible House), 225.

[2] Arthur W. Pink, *The Sovereignty of God* (Grand Rapids: Baker, 1969), 263.

[3] Merril F. Unger, *The New Unger's Bible Dictionary* (Chicago: Moody Press, 1988), 1214.

[4] James M. Boice, *Foundations of the Christian Faith* (Downers Grove, IL: InterVarsity Press, 1981), 120.

Chapter 3: The Dynamics of Grace

[1] R. C. Trench, *New Testament Synonyms,* cited by Kenneth S. Wuest, *Word Studies in the Greek New Testament,* vol. III (Grand Rapids: Eerdmans, 1973).

[2] Ibid.

[3] *Nelson's Illustrated Bible Dictionary,* Herbert Lockyer, ed. (Nashville: Nelson, 1986), 443.

[4] Boice, *Foundations of the Christian Faith,* 117.

[5] *Eerdmans' Handbook,* 548.

Chapter 4: Co-laboring with Grace

[1] Alan Richardson, ed., *A Dictionary of Christian Theology* (Philadelphia: Westminster, 1969), 148.

[2] Ray R. Sutton, *That You May Prosper* (Fort Worth: Dominion Press, 1987), 77.

Chapter 5: The Purpose of the Gifts

[1] Gordon D. Fee, *The New International Commentary on the New Testament, The First Epistle to the Corinthians* (Grand Rapids: Eerdmans, 1988), 686–687.

[2] Vine, *Expository Dictionary,* 111–112, 390.

[3] C. Peter Wagner, *Your Spiritual Gifts Can Help Your Church Grow* (Ventura, CA: Regal, 1979).

Chapter 6: An Overview of the Gifts

[1] Abraham Heschel, *The Prophets* (New York: Harper & Row, 1969), x, 25.

[2] Sinclair B. Ferguson and David F. Wright and J. I. Packer, eds., *The New Dictionary of Theology* (Downers Grove, IL: InterVarsity Press, 1988), 433.

[3] David K. Blomgren, *Prophetic Gatherings in the Church* (Portland, OR: Bible Temple Publications, 1979), 29.

[4] F. F. Bruce, *The New International Commentary on the New Testament, The Book of Acts* (Grand Rapids: Eerdmans, 1986), 425.

Chapter 7: The Internal Operation of Grace

[1] *The Interpreter's Bible,* vol. VIII, 182.
[2] *The American College Dictionary* (New York: Random House, 1964), 789.
[3] Bruce, *The Book of Acts,* 390.

Chapter 8: Creating the Atmosphere for Spiritual Gifts

[1] James Strong, *The New Strong's Complete Dictionary of Bible Words* (Nashville: Nelson, 1996), 448.
[2] Unger, *The New Unger's Bible Dictionary,* 872.

Chapter 9: Maturity and Variety of Spiritual Gifts

[1] Fee, *First Epistle to the Corinthians,* 582–587.
[2] Stanley Howard Frodsham, *Smith Wigglesworth, The Apostle of Faith* (Springfield, MO: Gospel Publishing House, 1948), 58–60.
[3] Mike Bickle, *Growing in the Prophetic* (Lake Mary, FL: Creation House, 1996), 150–159.

Chapter 10: How to Activate the Spiritual Gifts

[1] Frances J. Roberts, *Come Away My Beloved* (Ojai, CA: King's Farspan, 1973), 71.